WORLD
WAR II

TOP SECRET FILES

WORLD WAR II

STEPHANIE BEARCE

PRUFROCK PRESS INC.
WACO, TEXAS

Library of Congress Cataloging-in-Publication Data

Bearce, Stephanie.
Top secret files : World War II : spies, secret missions, and hidden facts from World War
II / by Stephanie Bearce.
    pages cm.
Includes bibliographical references.
ISBN 978-1-61821-244-3 (pbk.)
1. World War, 1939-1945--Juvenile literature. 2. Spies--Juvenile literature. I. Title.
D743.7.B43 2014
940.54'85--dc23
                                    2014011526

Copyright ©2015 Prufrock Press Inc.

Edited by Lacy Compton

Cover and layout design by Raquel Trevino

Background cover image courtesy of Keith Jones

ISBN-13: 978-1-61821-244-3

Prufrock Press Inc.
P.O. Box 8813
Waco, TX 76714-8813
Phone: (800) 998-2208
Fax: (800) 240-0333
http://www.prufrock.com

TABLE OF CONTENTS

SECRETS

SPIES

SPECIAL MISSIONS

SECRET WEAPONS

SECRET FORCES

SECRETS

Spy School

Ghost Army

CODE
I   II
B   CO
M   CMF
B   CO
B
B   H
B
B   KK CNCK
B
B

CODE
I   II
CO
CMF CO
H

B   KK CNCK
B
B
B

NFIDENTIAL

MINIATURE CAMERA

Churchill's Secret Army

Camp X

SPY ⊕
SCHOOL

    Great Britain was at war. Nazi Germany had invaded Poland and was marching across Europe with the hope of conquering every country in its path. Winston Churchill needed a new kind of agent to fight the Nazis. He needed people who could blow up bridges, steal weapons, break into buildings, and cause chaos for the German Army. So he created the SOE, the Special Operations Executive. The mission of the men and women of the SOE was sabotage, subversion, and guerrilla warfare done behind enemy lines. They would be taught how to parachute into enemy territory, send coded radio messages, and steal top secret plans from the Nazis. It would take intense training. It would take a school. A spy school.

Mansions and hunting lodges across Scotland and England were "borrowed" by the SOE to house the secret spy schools. Nobody was to know what was going on at the schools or why carloads of people were dropped off in remote parts of woods and bogs. The neighbors wondered and often correctly guessed that there was "something funny" going on, but for the most part, the schools stayed a secret, even from the people who owned the lands and homes.

Recruiting agents for the SOE was also top secret. Most of the new recruits didn't even know they were being interviewed to be an agent. They were brought into normal looking offices and questioned like it was a job interview. If they didn't pass the interview, they were just told they weren't right for the job. But if they did pass, they were told they were headed for SOE training school.

Training was broken into three different schools. The new recruits had to pass each school to get to the next. If they failed at any point, they were dismissed from the program. Being dismissed might mean being sent to a remote area of Great Britain to work on a farm for the rest of the war. Churchill didn't want anyone talking about what went on at spy school.

The very first test for a new agent was just getting to the school. The paramilitary training schools were located at 10 different hunting lodges scattered across Scotland. The new recruit was dropped off miles away from the lodge and told to walk the rest of the way. That little hike included slogging through muddy bogs, climbing craggy cliffs, and sometimes crawling through hedges or under wire fences. When the recruits arrived at the lodge muddy, scratched, and bleeding, they were told they had passed the first test. If they couldn't find the lodge, they got a free trip home.

Once they arrived at the paramilitary school, their training began in earnest. Physical training meant getting in shape just like regular soldiers. In addition to exercise, the recruits attended classes on bomb building and weapons handling. Men and women were taught how to shoot the Colt .45, Colt .38, and STEN guns. The STEN guns were British 9mm machine guns. Students were taught to fire from the hip rather than the way regular soldiers raised the gun and took aim. It may not have been as accurate, but it was faster, and speed was critical to staying alive. They were also told to fire twice so they had a better chance of hitting their target. It was called the double tap system and was unique to SOE agents.

Training was also given in knife fighting and bare hand combat. The agents were warned that they should never be without a weapon, but just in case they were, they needed to know street fighting techniques.

Explosive training was a requirement for every recruit, because sabotage was a high priority for SOE agents. The agents needed to know how to place explosives so they could take out a bridge or destroy a railroad. This would cause significant problems for the Nazi Army and slow them down in

Potential spy recruits in the classroom

Churchill tries a STEN gun like the ones spies were trained to use at Spy School

their march across Europe. The Scottish West Highland Rail Line agreed and allowed the students to practice placing fake explosive charges on their tracks and bridges. They even lent the school a train so the recruits could practice sabotage on a real locomotive and cars.

When the recruits had successfully completed their para-military training in Scotland, they were sent on to specialist training schools. Some of these schools were housed on the grounds of Lord Montague's estate, Beaulieu, in England. In specialist schools, the new agents were trained in subjects such as burglary. The teachers were often real burglars who had been released from jail under the condition they would teach their craft to SOE agents. The agents learned how to pick locks, crack safes, and steal from heavily guarded buildings. They also learned how to make copies of keys. They carried a matchbox that had been filled with a clay-like substance called Plasticine. When they pressed the key into the Plasticine, it made an impression and the copy was made from that impression.

Other SOE agents learned how to forge documents, make and decipher codes, operate portable radios, and blow up factories. Anything that would cause problems for the Nazi Army was taught and used by the SOE agents.

After they completed specialist training, the new agents had to learn parachute jumping. Almost all of the SOE agents were dropped behind enemy lines by parachute. Agents wore a small spade strapped to their leg for the purpose of burying their parachute and jump suit after they landed. Often the planes had to fly low to not be seen by radar. The low jumps were dangerous and if not done correctly, the agent could end up with broken bones. Trying to hide from the Nazis with a broken leg would *not* be a good way to start a mission.

Those who successfully completed jump school were ready for finishing school. This is where the agent was given his or her undercover identity. Agents had to memorize everything about this fake identity. It was critical both to their mission and to their life. They also needed to know everything about the country they were going into, otherwise they would stick out and be caught by the Nazis. Instructors taught the agents details about local customs, rationing, and railway timetables. Any small mistake could blow the agents' cover and get them captured.

Instructors warned students about one agent who forgot the lessons about rationing, went into a French café, and ordered a café noir (coffee black). It was a huge mistake. There was no cream available anywhere, so a local would have just said a café. The agent was immediately suspect by the Nazis and arrested.

Finishing school also taught the agents about disguises, but not the false beards and moustaches you might expect. Those were too easy to detect. Instead, agents were told to wear their hair differently, put on a hat, wear glasses, and walk with a different gait. Sometimes they did use make up and added scars to their face or hands with a substance called Culloden. It was waxy and could be molded into different shapes, but dried quickly.

If an agent really had his cover blown, there were plastic surgeons who would operate on the agent to change his face so he would not be recognized. SOE records show that several agents had to have plastic surgery. One brave Jewish agent underwent radical surgery to make his face look more German so that he could parachute back into Germany and continue bombing and destroying Nazi factories and railroads.

Once the agents finished all of their training, they were tested. They were given a pretend assignment to carry out in England. It might be placing fake explosives under a bridge or stealing files from a secure office. It could mean cracking a safe and clearing out the contents. They were supposed to complete their mission and return back to spy school without getting caught. But just in case a British policeman did catch them, they were given a secret phone number that the police could call and the arresting officer would be told to let them go because it was a matter of national defense.

The instructors believed the better students would never use the phone number and would argue their cover with the police. Often it worked, and the agents were released without ever having to call for help.

After the agents had received all of their training and their cover story, there was one more instruction: They were given two different pills that they were to keep on their person at all times. One was Benzedrine and was to be taken to keep the agent awake in emergency situations. The other was the "L" tablet. It was a suicide pill. If an agent bit down on the pill, he would be dead in 15 seconds. A dead agent could not be tortured for information. A dead agent would not betray other agents or his country.

Graduation from spy school meant being given an assignment. And the assignment for the SOE was always behind enemy lines. The agents were given a map, compass, and all of their equipment, including specially made clothes that would match what the ordinary citizens wore. They were not issued uniforms, and they knew they were not going to be recognized as a part of the military. If a soldier in uniform were captured, he would be sent to a prisoner of war camp. If a plainclothes person were caught, he would be tried as a traitor and executed.

Many of the SOE agents parachuted behind enemy lines at night, sometimes with a partner, but often alone. They would then have to make their way to their assigned site in the darkness, crawling under fences and rocky hills just like they had done to reach spy school in the first place.

Some of the SOE agents made it back to tell their stories. Many others died trying to stop the Nazis from killing the Jewish people and taking over Europe. Hundreds of successful SOE operations were carried out in every Nazi occupied country. In France, agents blew up a power station and damaged a German U-boat factory. In Czechoslovakia, an SOE hit squad assassinated one of Hitler's commanders, and in Greece, agents blew up a rail bridge and stopped supplies from getting to the Nazi Army. The SOE had a huge victory in Norway when SOE agents destroyed the heavy water plant at Vemork. That ended the Nazi's atomic bomb program. At the end of the war Prime Minister Winston Churchill was proud of his spy school and the men and women who served their countries by causing "chaos" for the Nazis.

BAREFOOT BOOTS
British secret agents usually wore shoes. But natives of the Pacific Islands went barefoot. To disguise their boots, British agents in the islands wore rubber soles on their boots that looked like bare feet, so all they left behind were **barefoot prints in the sand**.

Sir Winston Churchill

SECRET ARMY

It was 1940, and Hitler was marching across Europe. He had invaded Poland, Belgium, France, and the Netherlands. Winston Churchill feared that England was next. The only thing that stood between Hitler and England was the English Channel—and Churchill's secret army.

At the beginning of World War II, the Nazi Army had trapped the Allies at Dunkirk, France, and made the British retreat back to England. Prime Minister Churchill wanted to be sure that if Hitler invaded Britain, there would be resistance fighters trained and ready. So he began recruiting a secret army: men and women who would go about their normal daily jobs, but if there was an invasion, they would carry out Churchill's special orders.

Trevor Miners as a young Sargent in the Cadet Force with his parents

Trevor Miners was only 16 when he was recruited to be a part of the "Secret Army." Recruited by an intelligence agent, he signed the British Official Secrets Act and for more than 60 years, he told no one about his special mission.

"We were sent to a base in Oxfordshire," Miners said. "We were trained to kill, how to use a knife to kill a man quietly."

Trevor Miners, like the other men in the Secret Army, was assigned to a small resistance group of five or six other men. If there was an invasion, they were to quietly slip away from their friends and family and report to an underground bunker. The bunker was fortified with food and ammunition. They were supposed to seal themselves in the underground bunker for 30 days. This would allow Hitler and his army to think there was no resistance in Great Britain. After 30 days, all of the resistance groups were to emerge from their bunkers and start fighting the Nazis with whatever means possible.

They were trained in setting booby traps, how to build bombs, and how to handle a wide variety of weapons. Each local unit was given assigned targets. In case of invasion, they were expected to sabotage Nazi aircraft, trucks, tanks, and fuel stations. Some of the units were trained in radio operations and were expected to act as spies, reporting information back to British intelligence officers.

If they were ever captured, they were expected to take their own lives, rather than risk being taken alive, being tortured, and possibly betraying the resistance. Essentially, the Secret Army soldiers had signed up for a suicide mission. If the Nazis invaded, they had sworn to give their all to protect Great Britain.

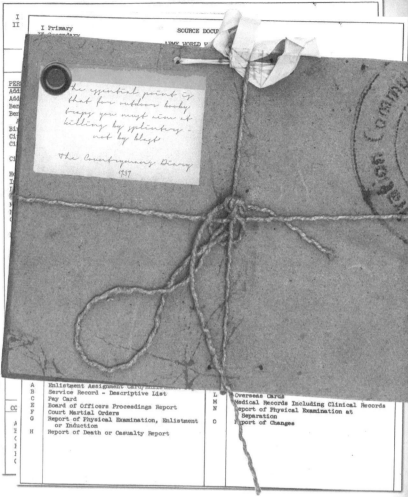

The essential point is that for outdoor booby traps you must aim at killing by splinters - not by blast.

The Countryman's Diary
1737

A	Enlistment Assignment	L	Overseas Cards
B	Service Record - Descriptive List	M	Medical Records Including Clinical Records
C	Pay Card	N	Report of Physical Examination at
E	Board of Officers Proceedings Report		Separation
F	Court Martial Orders	O	Report of Changes
G	Report of Physical Examination, Enlistment		
	or Induction		
H	Report of Death or Casualty Report		

Fortunately, the Secret Army was never called to action. By 1944, the Allies were winning the war and Prime Minster Churchill told his resistance fighters that they could "stand down." But most of the men and women who were willing to give their lives were never officially recognized. The secret of the resistance units was fiercely guarded—not generally made public knowledge until the 1990s, nearly 60 years after the end of the war.

GHOST

ARMY

The moon glowed as the Nazi Army leader crawled over the rough ground. His rifle was armed and ready. The men in his zugtrupp (platoon) followed, crawling silently behind. Just a few more yards and they would reach their target: an American battalion they had been spying on for days. The officer gave the signal, and the Nazis stormed in—ready to attack the unsuspecting Americans—but when they reached the target area, there was no army. No men. No tents. No trucks. Just an empty field with a few tire tracks. Where were the Americans they had heard on the radio? Where were the tanks their spies had just seen hours earlier? It was as if the army was made of ghosts . . . and they had just disappeared.

The 23rd Headquarters Special Troops were not a platoon of ghosts, but they happily accepted that nickname. Instead they were a troop of artists, actors, designers, and sound technicians recruited from Hollywood and various art schools. Their special mission was to confuse the German Army, and they became very good at it. The German soldiers called them the "Phantom Army" or "Ghost Army" because they would appear in one place, then mysteriously vanish, only to reappear to attack the Germans from behind. The Nazis could not understand how the Allies could move tens of thousands of soldiers so quickly.

In truth, the Ghost Army was made up of only a little more than 1,000 soldiers, and their weapons were fake balloon tanks, recordings of soldiers, and phony radio signals. Their assignment was to fool the Nazis into thinking a large army brigade was advancing in one direction, when in truth they were headed another way. The Ghost Army's job was to get the Germans to fire on them instead of launching an attack on the real military. These soldiers put their own lives on the line to try to save the lives of their comrades. It was a very dangerous job.

The Ghost Army used three major deceptions. The first was visual deceptions. This involved fake tanks, jeeps, trucks, and large guns all made of inflatable rubber. The soldiers would use air compressors or hand pumps to blow up the giant balloons, then they would place them in realistic positions to make it look like a real army camp. They even put camouflage on the fake tanks and trucks so it would look real to German spy pilots.

The sonic unit of the Ghost Army was in charge of sound deceptions. They recorded the noises of actual tanks moving, construction equipment running, and soldiers working. Then they put huge speakers on trucks, drove the trucks close to the enemy camp, and broadcast the sounds of the fake army. Any German spies listening in the area would swear that a military camp really existed.

The third deception was radio, and it was especially important. During World War II, radio waves were the main form of military communication. If there were no radio transmissions from the fake camp, the Germans would never be fooled, so skilled radio operators sent phony messages from the camp. Often they included "top secret" messages hoping the Nazis would believe they had intercepted critical intelligence. Of course, all of the "top secret" messages were false

DEATH BY NOISE

Have your parents ever said, "If you play that music too loud, you're going to go deaf?" Well, during WWII, Nazi scientists figured out a way to make sound so intense it could kill a person. The scientists took a recording of a methane gas explosion and used parabolic reflectors to make the sound so loud that it would shatter eardrums and kill a person from 150 feet away.

and would mislead the Germans if they believed them.

Sometimes the soldiers of the Ghost Army had to be actors. They would go into French towns and visit local pubs and restaurants. There, they would pretend to get drunk and tell important secrets. Any French citizens who were spying for the Nazis would report the information back to headquarters. This reinforced to the Germans that the camps were real.

The men also wore fake uniforms and sewed on fake patches for whatever battalion they were impersonating. Sergeants dressed up in general's uniforms and drove around the local towns talking about inspecting the troops.

In order to give the image of being a large battalion with thousands of men, they would drive army transport trucks back and forth all day long. They put two men at the very back of a covered troop transport truck. The rest of the truck would be empty but with the canvas cover pulled over the truck so that onlookers could not see inside. People assumed that it was a truck full of soldiers, but in reality there would only be two men and a driver in each truck.

Sometimes the soldiers ran into problems with their deceptions. One very hot summer day, the air heated up in the inflatable trucks and tanks and several of them exploded like giant parade balloons. When the weather cooled, the air would contract and the guns on the rubber tanks would droop. And sometimes the men would need to move a tank or a truck from one place to another. One day, two soldiers were not paying attention and lifted up a tank in front of two

French locals. The French men stood staring because they thought the men were lifting real tanks. The guard saw the men and told them that, "The American soldiers are very strong."

Success for the Ghost Army meant that they would be attacked. If they did a good job convincing the Germans that the fake camp was real, then the Germans would bomb the camp. During Operation Brest, the Ghost Army was to cover for the 6th Armored Division as it left the town of Brest and moved to another battlefield. The Ghost Army's inflated tanks, trucks, and guns fooled the Nazis and took more than 20 rounds of enemy fire. The real 6th Armored Division was not fired on during the entire move.

Their greatest success was Operation Viersen, where the Ghost Army was supposed to impersonate the 9th U.S. Army. Their job was to convince the Germans that the real 9th Army invasion was just a warm-up and that the bigger invasion was coming later. That way, the Nazis would hold back some of their military, and it would allow the Allies to successfully cross the Rhine river.

This took every single rubber tank and truck the army had. They inflated 5 airplanes, 10 howitzer guns, 88 tanks, and 250 trucks. They lined the perimeter of the camp with real trucks and weapons. The soldiers were not allowed to sleep during the whole operation because they had to keep airing up the dummy tanks and trucks and visiting the local villages to make it look like new troops were always coming in.

Operation Viersen was a great success. The 9th Army was able to cross the Rhine and defeated the Nazis. Lieutenant General W. H. Simpson sent a "Memorandum of Appraisal" to the Ghost Army officers praising them for their "attention to detail" and "diligent execution" of their tasks. The Ghost Army was so successful that it put itself out of a job. After

Operation Viersen, it became apparent to everyone that the United States would be victorious in the European War.

The Ghost Army was split up and sent to do a variety of work, but most of the men were assigned the task of helping take care of the nearly 100,000 people who had been captured by the Nazis. The Ghost Army soldiers helped provide the people with food, water, and transportation back to their native countries.

After the war, the soldiers of the Ghost Army could not talk about the work they had done. It was all top secret, and the records were not released until 1996. The men had to be silent for 40 years. Many of the soldiers from the Ghost Army went on to become famous artists, actors, and designers. Some of the famous soldiers were fashion designer Bill Blass, movie star Douglas Fairbanks Jr., artist Ellsworth Kelly, and fashion photographer Art Kane.

The soldiers of the Ghost Army liked to joke that when people asked them what they did during the war, they could honestly answer, "We blew up tanks and guns."

CAMP X

Camp X, a paramilitary and commando training installation in Whitby/Oshawa, Ontario, in 1943

President Roosevelt was worried. Reports from his operatives in Europe told about the horrible things that Adolf Hitler and the Nazis were doing to the Jewish people. Jewish families were arrested and sent to concentration camps where they were starved, abused, and forced into slave labor. Hitler and his army were fighting to conquer all of Europe and turn it into a German super country called the Third Reich, and Roosevelt could do nothing about it.

After World War I, the United States Congress had passed the Neutrality Act. This act stated that America would only participate in a war if the United States was attacked. In all other instances of war, the United States would remain neutral. Roosevelt knew that Europe needed help in fighting Hitler, but he also knew the law would not permit direct help. But Roosevelt *could* allow spies and saboteurs to go help

Europe, and he could get training for his own shadow army with a little help from his friends in Canada.

The Canadian government agreed to provide a secret place named Camp X for the British to prepare Canadian spies. They also agreed that any Americans who showed up at the camp could also train as spies. It was the beginning of a shadow army—a group of men and women trained in military tactics who were not recognized as being a part of the military. As a matter of fact, if they were caught, the military would deny they had ever heard of them.

It was a dangerous job. They would be trained as spies and sent in behind enemy lines, but they would not have the formal help or recognition of the United States. Still, men and women volunteered to help in the fight.

Frank Devlin was one of the first Americans trained at Camp X. He was given special orders that sounded like something out of a mystery novel. He was told to wear civilian clothes and take a train to Penn Station in New York City. From there, he was catch a train to Toronto, Canada. After he checked into the hotel, he was given a message with a secret number. That secret number was the license plate number for a car. He was told to get into the car and then he was driven out into the wilderness where Camp X was located. There he joined British and Canadian agents in training and began to learn the secrets of being a good spy.

A lot of the training for Camp X was in "night work." Spies were taught how to sneak into military camps, railroad stations, and buildings to plant bombs. One special type of bomb had an electric eye that activated when the train went into a tunnel. If the train exploded in the tunnel, it blocked the rail line for miles because none of the trains could get through the clogged tunnel. It was especially effective if the rescue train also had a bomb on it. It was really hard to clean up *two* exploded trains inside a tunnel.

Agents were also taught how to drive a locomotive. They practiced sneaking onto trains and capturing the controls. Once they had control of the train, they got it up to a high speed and jumped off. The runaway train would then wreck and cause rail lines to be disrupted. Stopping the shipment of guns and weapons by train would help cripple the Nazi Army.

The Camp X agents learned how to destroy power plants and poison water supplies. They learned how to ruin truck engines by putting sugar in the gas tanks and how to make explosives from simple household cleaning supplies. It would take only five or six agents from Camp X to cripple a medium-sized city.

Camp X was quite efficient at training agents, but the Americans only used it for a short time. When the Japanese attacked Pearl Harbor, the Neutrality Act was no longer in force and the United States entered into the war. Immediately President Roosevelt called for the formation of training camps in the United States.

Roosevelt selected Colonel William Donovan to head up the United States Office of Strategic Services (OSS). An abandoned boy's camp near Washington, DC, was selected to be the training camp for American spies and agents. Officially, the new training site was called Area B. Eventually it became Camp David and the OSS became known as the CIA (Central Intelligence Agency).

The OSS successfully accomplished missions in Europe, Africa, and Asia. The OSS Joes were agents who parachuted behind enemy lines and acted as undercover spies in enemy towns. They sent back maps, detailed battle plans, blueprints of military equipment, and ciphers for enemy codes. OSS Jedburgh teams had three men who were assigned the duties of organizing resistance fighters and sabotaging trucks, trains, factories, and planes. General Dwight D. Eisenhower, Supreme Commander of the Allied Forces, said the work done by the OSS agents helped shorten the war and saved countless lives.

Bond, James Bond

Author Ian Fleming was a spy-in-training at **Camp X**, but it was so overcrowded that he had to stay at a military residence in Toronto. Right across the street was the **Saint James Bond Church**. It was the inspiration for Fleming's famous novels about **super spy James Bond**.

SPY TRAINING

Spy Obstacle Course (SOC)

Spies need to be physically fit and able to get out of tight situations. You can practice your spy skills by creating a secret agent training course. All you will need are some everyday items, a large outdoor space, and permission from an adult.

Materials:

- ❑ String or rope
- ❑ Small posts or dowel rods
- ❑ Lawn chairs
- ❑ Balls
- ❑ Hula hoops

Your first job will be to scout out the area for your training course. A backyard or park is a good place. Remember that you will need to crawl over objects and under objects to show your skill as a spy.

Find an adult to help you set up the course. You can insert the posts or dowel rods into the ground and tie the rope in a zig-zag pattern to the posts. Set lawn chairs, balls, or hula hoops in your obstacle course. Show your spy recruits how to properly move through the obstacle course. Show them when they need to crawl under the rope and when they should climb over the rope. Use the chairs for them to run around or crawl through. Use your imagination to create a tricky course, but check with an adult to make sure your training course is safe. You don't want spy school to be shut down because of injuries!

SPY TRAINING
Rearview Glasses

Being a spy isn't easy. There's always a chance another spy could be following you. You need a way to see who is behind you, and that's why you need to make a pair of rearview glasses.

Materials:
- ❏ Inexpensive sunglasses
- ❏ Small mirror
- ❏ Super glue

They are simple to make. Just take an old pair of sunglasses and a small mirror from the dollar store, and super glue the mirror to the left side of the left glasses lens. With the help of the mirror, you will be able to look in your glasses and see who is right behind you.

THE WHITE MOUSE

The Nazis hated the spy they called "The White Mouse." This secret agent rescued hundreds of captured Allied soldiers and supplied the French resistance with thousands of guns and weapons. The Gestapo had tried everything they knew to find this dangerous spy. They tapped phone lines, spied on radio signals, and bribed people for information, but they weren't able to find the agent who could hide as easily as a little "white mouse." So they offered a reward of 5 million francs to anyone who could capture or kill the White Mouse. It still didn't work.

What the Gestapo didn't know was that the White Mouse was Nancy Wake, a young Australian journalist who had moved to France in the late 1930s. As a reporter, she had witnessed the cruel and horrible way the Nazis had treated German and Austrian Jews. She saw the Nazis chain and whip Jewish people and vowed that if she ever had a chance, she would fight against the Nazi regime.

Her chance came in 1940. While she and her husband, Henri Fiocca, were living in Marseilles, the Germans invaded France. Both Nancy and her husband joined the French Resistance. At first she worked as a courier delivering messages for resistance fighters. But soon she understood that, as the beautiful wife of a wealthy businessman, she could travel around the country with much less suspicion than many of the male spies. Nancy began helping Jewish refugees and Allied prisoners escape from France. She obtained false identification papers for them and even escorted the refugees as they crossed the Pyrenees Mountains into Spain. She helped more than a thousand people escape from France.

By 1943, the White Mouse was number one on the Gestapo's most wanted list. An acquaintance of Nancy's turned her in as a suspect and immediately Nancy's phone was bugged, her mail inspected, and she was followed wherever she went. Henri and Nancy agreed that it was time for her to leave Marseilles. Henri would stay behind and continue to work for the resistance. Nancy told Henri goodbye and

HIDE AND SEEK: THE MAQUIS

The Maquis (pronounced Ma' ki) took their name from the terrain where they hid. It was an area full of thickets and bushes. Roughly translated, Maquis Guerilla means bush fighters. They identified themselves by wearing a Basque beret. The Germans ignored the beret because they were common in French culture, but their fellow Frenchmen knew a Basque beret meant Maquis fighter.

then tried to follow the same path out of France she had taken with so many of her refugees.

It was not an easy trip for Nancy. She was captured and imprisoned twice, but escaped with help from other resistance fighters. Nancy was chased and shot at by German soldiers. She had to jump off a moving train, and nearly froze to death crossing the Pyrenees Mountains. It took seven tries before the White Mouse made it out of France. And once she was in England, all Nancy wanted to do was get back to fighting the Nazis.

She joined the SOE and was trained at a British Ministry of Defense Camp in Scotland. There she learned night parachuting, codes and radio operations, silent killing, and how to use guns, rifles, pistols, and grenades. Once her training was complete, Nancy parachuted right back into France. She became part of a team that included Major John Farmer and radio operator, Denis Rake. Their assignment was to connect with the French Maquis leaders and help them with supplies and munitions.

The Maquis were bands of fierce guerilla fighters who worked to sabotage the Nazi Army. With the help of direct radio contact with England, the agents in France could tell the British what supplies the Maquis needed. Then the British would tell Nancy and Major Farmer where the supplies would

Special Operations Executive: Nancy Wake's false identity papers be dropped. All transmissions were coded, and the codes were fiercely guarded.

Within a few months, Nancy was working with and supplying 17 different Maquis bands that included 7,000 men. Allied planes made night drops of weapons, ammunition, and money. Nancy delivered supplies and taught men how to use the weapons. She paid farmers for food so the Maquis would not have to steal to eat. The Maquis were heavily outnumbered by the Germans, but they were fierce fighters and often inflicted heavy damages on Nazi armies.

During one battle, Nancy's radio operator had to get rid of his radio and codebook so that it would not be confiscated by the Nazis. Without radio contact with England, the Maquis would soon run out of ammunition.

Don't Leave Home Without It

The critical weapon for a WWII spy was a radio. The B2 was the radio most often used by the French resistance. It could be hidden in a leather suitcase or wrapped in watertight containers and dropped by parachute and could transmit 500 miles. Only problem—it weighed 32 pounds. The Nazi Gestapo learned to watch for people lugging extra heavy suitcases around town.

The only way to alert the British and get new supplies was for someone to go to the closest radio operator and send a message for help. Nancy volunteered to go.

The French fighters tried to talk her out of it. The nearest radio was 200 kilometers away (125 miles). It would be dangerous for a woman to travel so far alone in the middle of a war. The Gestapo would stop her at check points, they would ask for identification papers that she didn't have, and she was a *woman*. Nancy said that as a *woman*, she would be less likely to be suspected as a spy, and she could pretend to be a housewife running errands, or if need be, she could flirt with the male guards. Nancy was given permission to go and set off for the journey on her bicycle.

She rode day and night through mountain terrain and country roads. She was stopped by Gestapo guards but was never detained. She managed to find the radio operator and return back to her camp, but it took more than 3 days and every ounce of strength she had. The bike had rubbed away all of the skin on her inner thighs, and she was so sore she could not sit or stand without pain. But it was all worth it. A new radio and set of codes arrived on the next parachute drop. The fight could go on.

Nancy continued to fight with the Maquis. She supervised parachute drops four times a week, organized and led raids on ammunition plants, and even led a raid on a Gestapo head-quarters in Montucon, France. During one raid, the White Mouse had to use her silent kill training to keep a sentry from alerting a guard and discovering her soldiers.

On August 25, 1944, Paris was liberated by the Allies. The White Mouse and her troops were celebrating in Vichy, France, when Nancy learned that her beloved husband, Henri, was dead. He had been captured by the Germans and tortured. The Nazis had executed him because he would not give them any information about his wife.

After the war, Nancy continued to work for the SOE in the intelligence department. She was awarded the George Medal from Britain, the Resistance Medal, Officer of the Légion d'honneur, and the Croix de guerre with two bronze palms and a silver star from France, and the Medal of Freedom from America. In 1960, she remarried an Englishman, John Forward, a former prisoner of war. She lived in Australia until 2001, when a widowed Nancy moved back to England. She died in 2011 at the age of 98. At her request, her body was cremated and her ashes were scattered over the French mountains where she fought with the resistance.

THE GADGET MAKER

Christopher Hutton

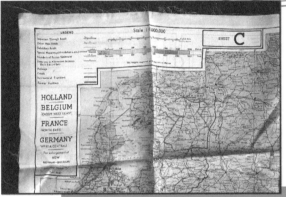

Silk Escape Map: The United States and Great Britain produced in excess of 3.5 million silk maps and cloth maps for Allied military personnel to use as escape maps. Hutton considered maps to be "the escaper's most important accessory."

Christopher Hutton was a magic buff and was especially fascinated with the escape artist Harry Houdini. When he was 20 years old and working at his uncle's lumberyard in West Midlands, England, he wrote a letter to Harry Houdini and challenged him to try to escape from one of the lumberyard's packing crates. Amazingly, Houdini showed up at the English lumberyard and accepted Christopher's challenge. Houdini even promised to give Christopher 100 British pounds if he couldn't break out of the packing box. It was more money that Christopher would make all year.

Houdini just asked for one small favor. He wanted to be able to meet with the carpenter who would build the box and inspect the crate himself. Of course, Houdini also posted bills advertising his show. Houdini was always looking for a paying audience. After Harry Houdini easily escaped from the packing crate, Christopher inspected the box and found that Houdini had bribed the carpenter to build an escape panel in the crate. Christopher learned that day that there was a trick to every escape.

That information would serve him well later in life. During World War I, Christopher served as an airplane pilot, and after the war, he worked as a journalist. When World War II broke out, Christopher wanted to help his country, but at the age of 37 was considered too old for combat service. He requested work as a military intelligence officer and ended up being hired by MI9, a section of British Military Intelligence that created evasion and escape gear for spies and soldiers.

Hutton created numerous gadgets that were to help soldiers and pilots if they were captured or shot down behind enemy lines. He is credited with the creating silk maps that pilots and aircrew carried. The silk was sturdier than paper, but it was lightweight. It could be folded or balled up to hide in a very tiny space and would not tear. If the soldier was able to evade capture, the map would lead him out of the enemy country. During the war, more than 400,000 escape maps were printed.

Hutton also designed special buttons that held tiny compasses that were sewn onto aircrew uniforms. And, he created special boots with detachable leggings that could be converted to look like civilian shoes. The heels were hollow and were stuffed with packets of dried food. He also designed an "escaper's knife" that held a strong blade, three small saw blades, a lock pick, screwdriver, and a wire cutter.

Hutton came up with an idea for how to smuggle escape equipment into prisoner of war camps. Charity groups often donated supplies and games to POW camps. This was permitted through the rules of the Geneva Convention. (Geneva Conventions are rules that tell countries at war how to treat wounded and captured enemy forces and enemy civilians. They were signed in Geneva, Switzerland, by representatives of many countries between 1864 and 1949.) The Nazis liked the packages because they helped keep prisoners calm and eliminate riots.

Christopher arranged for the makers of Monopoly to produce some special game boxes that were to be delivered to the POW camps. Before leaving for missions, British airmen were told that if they were captured they should watch for special-edition Monopoly boxes that had a red dot on the free parking space. Inside the box were a compass, escape knife, and real bank notes hidden under the fake money.

Over the course of the war, it is estimated that 35,000 men used Christopher's maps and tools to escape from enemy territory and return to Allied territory. These were escapes that outdid any of Harry Houdini's magic.

PIPE PISTOL

Smoking is bad for your health, but smoking a pipe pistol could be deadly. During WWII, British secret agents invented a pipe pistol that could actually shoot bullets while the user was smoking it. The pipe could shoot .22 caliber bullets through its stem, but it stayed in the lab and was never used in the war.

PRINCESS SPY

She was beautiful and smart, but nobody ever though Noor Inayat Khan would be a good spy. As a young woman, she studied art and music at the University of Sorbonne in France and wrote and illustrated children's stories. Noor was the great-great-great-granddaughter of the royal Tipu Sultan of India and a well-educated princess. But a spy? Never. She was just too timid and gentle. How could she ever stand up to the Nazis?

But Noor abhorred Hitler's tyranny over the Jews and wanted to fight the German Reich. She had witnessed the cruel way the Nazis treated the Jewish people and wanted to stop them. She joined the British Women's Auxiliary Air Force (WAAF) and trained as a radio operator. Fluent in both English and French, Noor was soon recruited by the SOE. With her radio and language skills, the SOE thought she might be able to work as a radio operator behind enemy lines in France. But Noor failed her fake Gestapo interrogation when she was woken in the dead of night, drenched in cold water, and questioned. If she couldn't withstand a fake interrogation, what would happen if she was really caught by the enemy? Would she give up secret information? Would she tell the names of other spies? Many of her instructors thought Noor was just too frail and shy to be a spy.

However, Noor was extremely talented at quick radio transmissions and the SEO was desperate for radio operators. Against the instructors' recommendations, the head of the unit decided to send Noor to Paris to help the French resistance. In June of 1943, Noor was given the cover name Nora Baker and was flown during the night to Nazi-occupied France. Her assignment was to join the Prosper radio operator's network. She would send and receive coded messages from the Allies in Britain. The messages would tell of Nazi troop movements and arms information. In order to keep from being caught, Noor and the other radio operators had to be constantly on the move. The Nazis had their own spies listening for radio transmissions and would capture and kill anyone they caught spying.

The Germans were using a device called a "listening machine." They hid their machine in vans disguised as laundry vans, bakers' vans, or repair vans. They assumed any identity they thought would be a good cover. This meant the Allied radio operators had to travel to a different place every time they needed to make a transmission. Tiny Noor had to carry a

Roald Dahl
Author/Spy

Ever heard of *Charlie and the Chocolate Factory* or read the book *James and the Giant Peach*? Believe it or not, before Roald Dahl wrote his famous children's books, he was a British spy. If he was caught or questioned, he always made up a good story. Maybe those spy stories are what helped him dream up such amazing books.

30-pound radio set in a suitcase and act like it was a lightweight bag of clothes so she would not attract attention.

Ten days after Noor arrived, the Germans arrested all of the Allied radio transmitters in Paris. Noor was not detected, perhaps because she was so new. The arrests left Noor as the only allied radio operator in Paris. Noor may have been scared but she never admitted it to her supervisors in England. They told her she should get out, but Noor bravely stated that she knew she was their only source of information. She volunteered to stay.

For 12 weeks, Noor moved from house to house setting up her radio and transmitting coded messages. She was the only radio operator able to give the Allies any information about the Nazi movements in Paris. She had several narrow escapes. Twice she was stopped by the Gestapo and asked about her bag. She told them she was carrying a movie projector. Her supervisors back in England knew she was under investigation by the Gestapo and again told Noor to get out, but she refused to leave until they sent a replacement for her.

Unfortunately, one of Noor's French acquaintances agreed to betray her to the Nazis for 100,000 Francs. Noor returned to her apartment and was met by a Nazi officer. He attempted to arrest the petite Noor and found out that she was not going without a fight. Noor fought tooth and nail and eventually the officer had to call for help. When additional officers arrived, they found that the arresting officer was bleeding heavily from the wounds Noor had inflicted.

Once in prison, Noor was determined to escape. When she was supposed to be taking a bath, she climbed through the bars of her cell and ran across the rooftop. The guards caught her and brought her back. Later, she worked with two other prisoners who had hidden a screwdriver in their cell. They chiseled away at the cement around the bars on their window until the bars were loose. Then they managed to escape to the roof, but at that time air raid sirens went off and searchlights flashed over the roof. Noor and her fellow spies were found and dragged off the roof.

While she was in prison, Noor and several other women prisoners managed to exchange messages by scratching words into the bottom of their food bowls. Noor was interrogated and tortured, but she never gave the Germans any information. Her SEO supervisors would have been surprised and proud. Because of her multiple attempts at escape and her tendency to fight her guards, Noor was deemed a dangerous prisoner and was scheduled to be sent to the high security prison of Dachau. Noor was able to send one last message to her fellow inmates. She scratched into her food bowl, "I am leaving." It was the last message Noor ever sent.

Noor and three other female British agents were executed in Dachau. Their bodies were burned so there would be no trace of them. But the Allies did not forget Noor and her brave work. After the war, France awarded her the Croix de guerre (Cross of War) and Great Britain gave her the George Cross, Britain's highest award for courage somewhere other than the battlefield.

Every Bastille Day (July 14), a French military band plays outside the childhood home of Princess Noor Inayat Kahn to honor the courage of this gentle woman who turned out to be one of the toughest agents of the SEO.

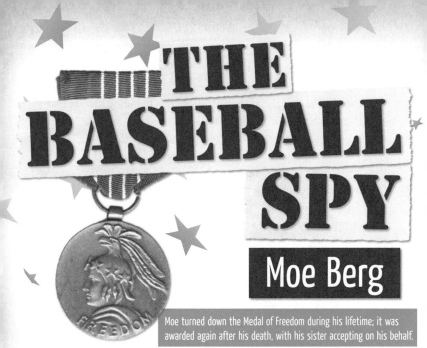

THE BASEBALL SPY

Moe Berg

Moe turned down the Medal of Freedom during his lifetime; it was awarded again after his death, with his sister accepting on his behalf.

Moe Berg loved baseball. He played in the major leagues for 15 years and personally knew baseball legends like Babe Ruth, Lou Gehrig, and Lefty Gomez. He was also a spy.

Moe started playing baseball when he was a little boy in Newark, NJ. He went on to play for the Princeton University's baseball team while getting his degree in modern languages. He studied Latin, Greek, French, Spanish, Italian, German, and Sanskrit. Sometimes when he was playing first base, Moe and the second baseman would communicate the plays in Latin. It confused the other team and gave Princeton the advantage. When Moe graduated from college in 1923, he signed a contract to play shortstop for the Major League Brooklyn Robins.

As much as Moe loved baseball, he also loved learning. During the off-season, Moe studied law at New York's Columbia University. He kept up on world events and read 10 newspapers every day. He graduated from law school, passed the New York Bar exam, and worked for a Wall Street law firm, all during the time he was playing Major League baseball.

Moe was never considered a top-tier player. He was good at fielding and set an American League record of 117 consec-

Spy for the Office of Strategic Services

utive errorless games, but he couldn't hit. His lifetime batting average was .243. When Washington Senators' outfielder Dave Harris was told that Moe could speak seven different languages, he shook his head and said, "Yeah, I know, and he can't hit in any of them."

So why was a mediocre baseball player asked to join a group of All-Stars on a trip to Japan in 1934? Was it because he was assigned a job as a spy? Moe traveled to Japan with Babe Ruth and Lou Gehrig to play exhibition games. While he was there, he gave a welcome speech in Japanese, spoke to the Japanese Legislature, and went to the hospital to visit the daughter of American Ambassador Joseph Grew. Only the ambassador's daughter never saw him. Instead, Moe sneaked onto the roof of the hospital and filmed the city and harbor with his movie camera. Moe never explained why.

After 15 seasons as a player, Moe worked as a coach for the Boston Red Sox during the 1940 and 1941 seasons. Then on December 7, 1941, Pearl Harbor was bombed by the Japanese and America was thrown into World War II.

Moe wanted to serve his country. He was hired by Nelson Rockefeller's Office of Inter-American Affairs. He was given the official duty of monitoring the health and physical fitness of the American soldiers stationed in South America, but in reality, Moe used his language skills to travel around South America and learn all he could about threats to the United States.

After he completed his mission in South America, Moe was hired by the United States Office of Strategic Services (OSS). He used his athletic skills to parachute into Yugoslavia and then worked with resistance fighters who were fighting the Nazis.

Next, Moe was sent to Italy. His top secret assignment was to try to kidnap Italian rocket and missile scientists and bring them to the United States. While he was working in Europe, the OSS sent him on his most dangerous mission. They equipped him with a gun and a cyanide pill. If he was caught, Moe was to take the pill and kill himself. No one was to find out his assignment.

Moe traveled to Zurich, Germany, to attend a lecture by the famous Nazi scientist, Werner Heisenberg. Because Moe spoke fluent German, he could blend in with the other scientists in the audience. Moe was told to find out how close the Germans were to developing an atomic bomb. If Heisenberg said anything that made Moe believe the Germans were close to completing a bomb, he was to shoot Heisenberg.

Moe sat in the lecture hall with a gun hidden under his jacket and a cyanide pill at the ready. But as he listened, he came to believe that the Nazis were not close to building an atomic bomb. Moe left the lecture without having to fire the shot.

For the rest of the war, Moe traveled throughout Europe completing different missions for the OSS. After the war, Moe never talked about his assignments and never wrote an autobiography. No one but Moe Berg knows exactly what else he did during his time in Europe.

He spent the rest of his life quietly studying. He was reclusive and spent much of his time reading his newspapers. He never married and lived with his sister until his death at the age of 70. To the very end, he loved baseball. His final words were, "How did the Mets do today?" They won.

DOUBLE AGENT
GARBO

Joan Pujol Garcia spent time working in a hardware store, a movie theater, and even trained to be a chicken farmer, but the job he was really good at was spying. Born in 1912 in Barcelona, Spain, Pujol witnessed the horrors of the Spanish Civil War. His mother and sister were imprisoned and accused of being counter-revolutionaries and Pujol himself spent time in a Nationalist prison. He was emphatic that neither communism nor fascism were good for anyone and decided that he would fight against them both.

When war broke out in 1940, Pujol decided he wanted to make a contribution "for the good of humanity" and offered himself as a spy for Great Britain. The British had no idea who this man was. They thought he was probably a spy sent from Germany and refused to work with him. Pujol was disappointed but he didn't give up.

He worked out a plan to infiltrate the German spy system and then go back to the British and offer to be a double agent. Pujol made up a new identity. He posed as a pro-Nazi who worked for the Spanish government. He obtained a forged passport and documents that convinced the Germans that he worked for the Spanish embassy in Lisbon, Portugal. The Germans hired him.

They trained him in espionage, gave him a bottle of invisible ink, a codebook, and about 600 pounds (the equivalent of $3,000 American dollars, a large sum of money in that day). Pujol was ordered to move to Britain and recruit more spies. Pujol had no intention of going to Britain; he didn't even speak English well. Instead he went to Lisbon and checked out English travel guides from the library.

By watching British newsreels and reading travel guides, newspapers, and magazines, Pujol was able to create convincing spy reports. He told the Nazis he was traveling around Great Britain recruiting new spies. He even turned in expense reports based on train fares published in an English railway guide.

The Nazis were convinced that Pujol was a legitimate spy and they were ecstatic when they received the news that he had indeed recruited three new spies—one in Liverpool, one in Glasgow, Scotland, and one in Western England. The whole time, Pujol was radioing the information from his apartment in Lisbon.

The information Pujol was sending the Nazis was mostly fiction with enough harmless facts to make the reports believable. He told about troop movements across the English countryside and mentioned a variety of military units. He gave detailed information on his pretend recruits and sent their reports, too.

Meanwhile the British Intelligence Agency MI-5 was going crazy. Who was this mysterious Nazi spy and where was he? The British had successfully rounded up most of the Nazi spies in the country, and had even turned some of them into double agents. But this spy was a mystery. How had this spy slipped through their intense security system?

About this time, Pujol became nervous. He was running out of information that could be found in the Lisbon Library.

Tank landing ships unloading supplies on Omaha Beach, preparing for the break-out from Normandy. The double agent code named "Garbo" developed a fake network of informants to convince the Germans that the attack would come in July to Calais.

He was afraid his hoax was about to fall apart, so he once again contacted the Allies. This time the Allies were interested. On April 24, 1942, British Intelligence moved Pujol to England and gave him the code name Garbo. He was named after the famous actress Greta Garbo, because Pujol was so good at acting like a spy.

Within a few months of arriving in England, Pujol (Garbo) was sending hundreds of messages to the Nazis. The Germans were so impressed with Pujol and his spy network that they didn't bother trying to recruit anyone else in Great Britain. With Pujol's help, the Allies were able to convince the Nazis that the large-scale invasion planned for D-Day was going to occur at Pas de Calais rather than at Normandy. Pujol was so successful that 3 days after the real Normandy invasion, the Nazis still had two armored divisions waiting for the pretend invasion at Pas de Calais.

The Nazis never knew that their number one spy had been a number one fake. In July of 1944, Pujol was awarded the Iron Cross Second Class for his services to the German War effort. The award was given over radio channels and the medal was delivered to Pujol by one of his German handlers. The Nazis even paid all of Pujol's fake spies. Pujol received

Code Name:
ZIG-ZAG

Zig-zag was the code name for double agent Eddie Chapman. Before the war, he spent time in prison for safe cracking. The Germans recruited him to blow up an English airplane factory, but instead he surrendered to the Allies and volunteered to be a double agent. He was called Zig-zag because he changed sides so many times no one knew what direction he would go next.

an amazing sum of $340,000 in U.S. currency—a fortune in that time period. King George VI awarded Pujol the MBE (Member of the Most Excellent Order of the British Empire) in November of 1944. Pujol became one of the few spies to ever receive awards from both sides of the war.

At the end of WWII, Pujol was worried that if the Nazis ever found out what he had done they would torture and kill him. So with the help of the British MI5, Pujol faked his death. The Nazis believed he had died of malaria, and Pujol moved to Lagunillas, Venezuela, where he ran a bookstore.

It wasn't until 1984, nearly 40 years after the war, that the world learned of Agent Garbo and his amazing spying. Author Rupert Allason researched and found the mysterious agent Garbo. He convinced Pujol to travel to London, where he met with Prince Phillip, visited the Special Forces Club, and was reunited with friends from his days as a spy. On the 40th anniversary of D-Day, Pujol went to Normandy to see the sight of his biggest success as a double agent. He died in 1988 at the age of 76 and is still regarded one of the greatest spies of the war.

JOSEPHINE BAKER

Flag of the French Resistance

Josephine Baker was a star. She sang and danced in France to rooms full of faithful fans. She starred in movies, sang opera, and was the most photographed woman of 1926. Smart and glamorous, Josephine was the darling of French society, but when Hitler marched into her beloved France, she became a spy.

Born in St. Louis in 1906, she grew up in deep poverty and spent 3 years living on the streets. Her one joy in her youth was dancing. She loved peeking in theatres and watching the young women dance to the new style jazz music. She practiced every dance step she saw until she had perfected it and then she added some moves of her own. She danced on the street corners and collected the change people threw to her. Eventually she was hired to be one of the dancers on the stage. Her energetic dancing stood out from the other dancers and got her noticed. When show producers from France offered her a chance to perform abroad, Josephine was ready for the adventure.

Paris was a whole new world for Josephine. The Parisian audiences did not discriminate against her for being African American. They thought she was lovely and exotic. She became the most popular singer and dancer in the whole country. She also became quite wealthy.

Eventually Josephine decided to become a French citizen and gave up her U.S. citizenship. She had traveled back to visit America and found that people were still not ready to treat African Americans with respect. Josephine was very happy in her new country and was horrified when the Nazis invaded in 1940.

Josephine had toured Europe and had performed on stage in front of German audiences. When she was in Germany, the newspapers reported that they thought it was shameful to have a Black performer on the same stage with white Aryan dancers. Some audiences yelled insults at Josephine and others threw things at the stage, including ammonia bombs.

After that tour, Josephine always saw the Nazis as being racist. On November 9, 1938, she was even more appalled when she heard about Kristallnacht (Night of Broken Glass). That was the night Nazis all over Germany attacked and destroyed Jewish homes, cars, synagogues, and businesses. At that moment, Josephine vowed to do whatever she could to defeat the Nazis. She joined the International League against Racism and Anti-Semitism, and her convictions were noticed by people in the French Resistance.

At first, some officials in the resistance movement thought it would be ridiculous to ask a female singer and dancer to act as a spy. What did a famous actress know about hardship? Would she be loyal if she were captured or questioned? The officials obviously didn't know Josephine Baker.

When Captain Jacques Abtey, the chief of counter intelligence in Paris, interviewed her, Josephine said, "France has made me what I am . . . They have given me everything, especially their hearts. Now I will give them mine. Captain, I am ready to give my life for France. You can make use of me as you will."

Josephine was hired and given the title of "honorable correspondent." She received training in weapons handling, self-defense, espionage, and languages. Then she started her work as a spy.

Because she was such a famous performer, she was allowed to freely travel all over France and in and out of the country. She became a courier, hand-carrying messages from one occupied region to another. She also attended many parties and functions where there were high-ranking Nazi officials. Nobody thought that the laughing, flirting dancer was actually listening for information on troop movements and secret operations.

Sometimes Josephine would excuse herself to go to the powder room. While there, she would jot down notes on what she heard and hide the notes in her underwear. Other times, she would write information in invisible ink on the margins of her song sheets. She could easily pass the music sheets on to another agent who posed as a singer or band player.

Josephine even used her chateau in the French countryside to hide Jewish refugees and helped smuggle them out of Nazi territory. When the Nazis in France became suspicious, Josephine went on tour to "entertain the troops." Captain Abtey came along and posed as her "personal secretary." She began performing in Spain, Portugal, and North Africa—all the while helping resistance fighters in those countries and passing back military secrets to her supervisors.

At the end of World War II, Josephine was recognized for her spy work and was awarded the French Croix de guerre (Cross of War), the Légion d'honneur, and Rosette of the Resistance. She continued to perform as a singer and dancer around the world and fought for racial equality everywhere she went. In the 1950s and 1960s, she became involved in the fight for equal rights in America and spoke at the 1963 March on Washington. Her speech was just before Martin Luther King's "I Have a Dream" speech.

She died in Paris at the age of 68. She was still dancing and singing on stage just 4 days before her death. When she was buried, her adopted country showed their gratitude—she was given a funeral with full military honors.

SPY TRAINING

Fingerprint Kit

Identifying an enemy spy is often the way to keep yourself and your country safe. One way to identify people is through their fingerprints. Every person has a unique fingerprint. Even twins don't have the same fingerprints; they have a mirror image of each other's prints.

Materials:

- ❏ Colored chalk
- ❏ Mortar or masher
- ❏ Cornstarch
- ❏ Clear tape
- ❏ Magnifying glass
- ❏ Make-up brush
- ❏ Plastic container
- ❏ Ink pad

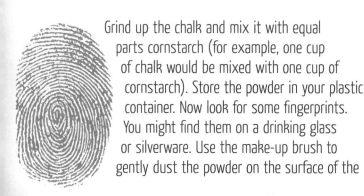

Grind up the chalk and mix it with equal parts cornstarch (for example, one cup of chalk would be mixed with one cup of cornstarch). Store the powder in your plastic container. Now look for some fingerprints. You might find them on a drinking glass or silverware. Use the make-up brush to gently dust the powder on the surface of the glass or silverware. The dust will adhere to the oils in the fingerprint, rendering it visible. You can lift the print off of the glass with a piece of clear tape. Look at the fingerprint with the magnifying glass.

In order to know who was drinking from that glass, you will need to fingerprint your suspects. Ask the people you suspect to let you fingerprint them with the inkpad. Record their fingerprints on a piece of paper. Then use your magnifying glass to match the prints to see who was using that glass. Once you have practiced, you will be able to solve real mysteries, like which one of your sisters or brothers got into your chocolate stash. Or was it your sneaky Mom instead?

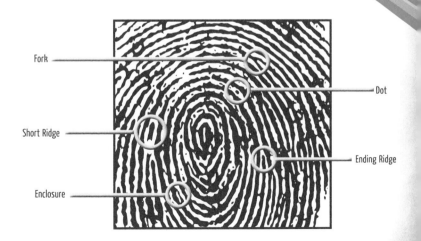

Fork

Dot

Short Ridge

Ending Ridge

Enclosure

Name That Spy

Having a fake identity is essential to being a spy. You need to create a new name, address, job, birthday, and even a fake family. It's not easy keeping all that information straight. That's why spies sometimes make their fake names from an anagram.

Anagrams are a type of word game where the letters of a word or phrase are rearranged to make a new word or phrase. Spies take the letters of their first and middle names or the letters of their hometown and turned it into a new name for their secret identity.

For example: Elizabeth Ann can be rearranged to make the spy name Theanna Beliz or Darrell Ray can turn into Larry L. Read.

See if you can create your own spy identity with the letters from your name. Once you have your secret agent name you can fill out your official Spy Identification Card.

IDENTITY CARD

No. ....

Name of Holder..

Place of residence..

Place of business..

Occupation..

Date of birth...Place of birth............................

Place photo here

Height.............................feet...inches

Color of eyes.........................Color of hair...

Signature of issuing officer...

Place...Date...............................

SPECIAL MISSIONS

The Allies were trapped. The German forces had surrounded the British and French troops and were advancing against them. The Allies literally had their backs to the ocean. More than 400,000 men were trapped with no way out. It was a disaster.

On May 19, 1940, British Commander Lord Gort called for retreat. The British Navy was called in to try to rescue some of the troops, but with Hitler's planes dropping bombs from the sky and Nazi tanks rolling forward, it looked desperate. Worse, the French sea town of Dunkirk was a shallow port, so shallow the large Navy vessels could not get close to shore. The soldiers that weren't killed on land would drown trying to swim so far out to sea.

There was only one choice—to use "Operation Dynamo." The British Navy might not have shallow water boats, but the British people did. As an island nation laced with rivers, the British people owned many pleasure boats, private yachts, commercial fishing boats, and flat-bottomed ferries. These boats were made for shallow water and could get in close to the shore.

A message went out on the British radio. The Admiralty asked all owners of pleasure craft to send their boats to their local officials. It may have sounded like a request, but it was an order, and hundreds of loyal British citizens responded. Fishermen donated their workboats, millionaires sent their yachts, and ferry captains volunteered their boats. Navy officers were ordered to scour the banks of the Thames river and confiscate any boat they believed could be useful to the evacuation. The military tried to find the owners of the boats, but if the owners could not be found, they took the boats anyway. It was a national emergency. King George VI called for a day of prayer. The churches of Britain were filled to overflowing. The whole nation was determined to help any way they could.

But even with the help of the "little ships," it was feared that most of the army would be lost. British Prime Minister Winston Churchill later stated that he had hoped that they could save 30,000 men. He was afraid they were going to lose more than 350,000 soldiers. If that happened, the war would be over and Hitler would rule all of Europe. But the British people weren't ready to give up. More than 700 little ships answered the call. And with them came retired soldiers and volunteer sailors. They were determined to "bring their boys home."

The Navy equipped the little ships with a full tank of fuel and a sea chart. They were told to head to Dunkirk, France, and they would get further directions when they arrived. But when the ships arrived, what they saw was the black smoke of bombs and fires. The Nazi planes kept dropping bombs and guns fired from the shore. The British Royal Air Force tried to defend the little ships. Their spitfires zipped through the skies fighting with the German Luftwaffe planes.

The first of the "little ships" arrived on May 28. The soldiers still had to wade out to waist-deep water to get on the boats and then the ships took the soldiers out to the large warships waiting in the ocean. The Germans kept bombing—many of the ships were hit and more than 100 of the little ships were sunk. Some boats made one or two trips before they were hit. Some made as many as nine trips from the shore to the boats.

Churchill watched anxiously for reports from Dunkirk. Each day the numbers of dead increased, but so did the numbers of rescued soldiers. For 8 days, volunteer captains and their little ships kept working, moving as many men as they could hold to the "big" ships waiting in the ocean. On June

4, the last ship was ordered to pull out of Dunkirk. Churchill nervously waited to hear the total number of soldiers saved. He had hoped to save 30,000 men, but the British people and their little ships had rescued 338,226 men. Churchill called it "The Miracle of Dunkirk" and declared that the little ships and their owners had saved the British Army.

PROJECT 19

It was 1941, and the Nazis were shooting Allied planes down faster than the English could repair them. It was a disaster. But Winston Churchill had an idea. With the secret cooperation of President Roosevelt and American aircraft companies, Boeing and Douglas, they built a secret repair site in North Africa. **Hundreds of mechanics sailed from the United States to Africa and spent 18 months working on Project 19.** They repaired the planes so fast and so well that the Nazis called for retreat in Africa before the United States ever officially entered the war.

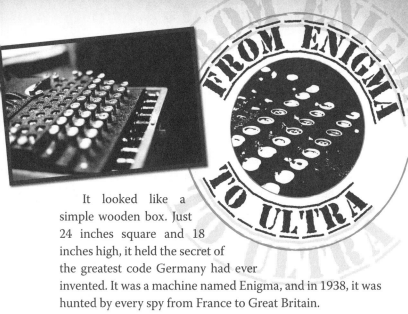

It looked like a simple wooden box. Just 24 inches square and 18 inches high, it held the secret of the greatest code Germany had ever invented. It was a machine named Enigma, and in 1938, it was hunted by every spy from France to Great Britain.

Writing in code or cipher was nothing new. It had been going on for thousands of years. Archeologists have found clay tables from 1500 BCE that were written in code, and the Romans used a code called the Caesar cipher. But until the Enigma machine, codes and ciphers had to be written and decoded by hand. It was a time-consuming method and could take hours for a complicated code. The Enigma machine was battery powered and could accomplish the same job in 2 or 3 minutes. Plus it could create 22 billion different code combinations. The Germans had an unbreakable code.

The Enigma machine looked like a typewriter with rotating wheels. The keys were connected through intricate wiring to those wheels. When a cipher clerk typed in a message, the wheels would rotate and the connections would change each time. This meant that the codes changed every time the machine was used. To decipher the code, you had to know where the typist had set the wheels at the beginning. Without that information, it was hopeless.

As early as 1938, France and Great Britain both realized that Adolf Hitler was about ready to start a war. Hitler wanted to expand German lands and eliminate the Jewish people. It was critical that countries around Germany be able to learn what the Nazis had planned. The British intelligence agency believed their best hope of cracking the German code was to steal an Enigma machine.

Finally in 1939, British agents made contact with the Polish Secret Service. The Poles knew where there was a German factory that built Enigma machines and they already had some agents working undercover in the factory. It took the Polish agents several days, but they were able to smuggle one of the machines out of the factory and to Warsaw. How they managed to get the 30-pound box out of the building without being caught was something of an espionage miracle.

British agent Commander Alastair Denniston snuck into Poland to pick up the enigma machine and transported it back to London. Mathematicians and scientists from England, Poland, and France studied the machine and decided that the only way they could break the Enigma code was to build a super code machine of their own. All three countries agreed that the research and building of the machine had to be done in Great Britain because there was a strong chance that Hitler could invade either Poland or France immediately. So on July 24, 1939, all of the information that Poland and France had about Enigma was given to the British Secret Service.

As soon as the Enigma machine reached London, a team of mathematicians and scientists set up a laboratory in an old mansion in the small town of Bletchley Park. These scientists worked frantically to figure out a way to build a machine that could match the electrical circuits of the Enigma machine. They knew that time was critical and lives could be saved or lost by breaking the Enigma code.

On September 1, 1939, Germany invaded Poland. The German air force, called the Luftwaffe, bombed Polish cities and German battleships attacked the Baltic Sea town of Danzig. In a few short weeks, there were 66,000 dead in Poland and 694,000 people were captured and imprisoned.

The scientists at Bletchley Park had been working day and night for 6 weeks. Two days after Germany invaded Poland, the scientists had a breakthrough. The machine they built, called Bombe, could match the circuitry of Enigma. On September 3, 1939, Great Britain declared war on Germany. Throughout the war, the scientists, code breakers, and mathematicians used Bombe to decode German messages and learn the German plans for their attacks. The Germans never knew their unbreakable code had been broken. They continued to send messages using their Enigma machines. The code breakers at Bletchley Park worked furiously to decipher every message that was sent. The code-breaking system was named Ultra, and it helped the Allies win the war.

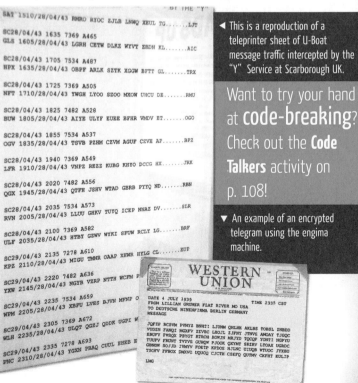

◄ This is a reproduction of a teleprinter sheet of U-Boat message traffic intercepted by the "Y" Service at Scarborough UK.

Want to try your hand at **code-breaking**? Check out the **Code Talkers** activity on p. 108!

▼ An example of an encrypted telegram using the engima machine.

Site X was a town that didn't exist, a city so top secret it couldn't be listed on any map in America. People who lived in the town pledged to never talk about their work, not even with their husbands or wives. It was such a top secret town that it was surrounded by a fence with guard towers and everyone had to have special identification papers to get in. Even the children had to wear I.D. badges and be searched each morning before they entered school.

Even the people who lived at Site X didn't exactly know what they were doing at their jobs. They just knew that they were working on a project that could end the war and help the Allies defeat Hitler and Japan.

Site X was located in the valley of the Clinch River near Knoxville, TN, and was home to a critical part of the top secret Manhattan Project. What the people of Site X didn't know was that they were working in a uranium enrichment plant, helping to build the world's first nuclear bomb.

As soon as President Roosevelt gave the okay for the Manhattan Project, Major General Leslie Groves began to hunt for the perfect place to build the uranium factory. He chose the Tennessee valley because it was remote and had a very low population—the fewer people who knew what was going on, the better. And the valley itself was protected on each side by several mountain ridges. If there was an accident at the nuclear plant, the mountains would help contain the damage.

Of course, most of the people hired to work at the plant had no idea how dangerous their work really was. Workers were given just enough detail to do their own job well and

"Stay on the job" rally at J.A. Jones Construction Co. in Oak Ridge, TN.

were told never to ask about anyone else's jobs. The military did not want any hint getting back to the Nazis that the U.S. was working on a nuclear weapon. Workers' mail and phone calls were all monitored and people were told that it was their duty to report anyone who talked about their work. Huge billboards all around town reminded people that "loose talk helps our enemy," "keep your trap shut," and any information you know "leave it here."

The military knew that refining enough uranium to make an atomic bomb would take a huge factory and thousands of workers. Once Site X was chosen, they began construction of the town and plant and hired 78,000 people to work in a town that didn't even exist. Scientists were hired from universities across the United States. They were not told what the project was about, only that they would be working with uranium. They were not to ever say the word uranium, but instead to use the code word Tuballoy. Secretaries, factory workers, nurses, new high school graduates, and college students were given lie detector tests they had to pass before they were hired to work in the secret city. They left their homes and families and were not to tell them where they were going. Then, they spent the next 3 years working for the government.

Some scientists and workers brought their families. The military hired builders to construct houses, schools, and municipal buildings. The construction was done so fast that, at one point, they were putting up a new house every 30 minutes. Within a few short months, Site X had 17 restaurants, 13 supermarkets, 10 schools, seven theatres, a library, and a

Woman welding at K-25 in February 1945.

symphony orchestra. The new residents of the top secret city voted to name the town Oak Ridge, but it was not until 1949, 5 years after the end of the war, that Oak Ridge was added to the maps of Tennessee.

On August 6, 1945, newspapers and radios across America announced that the United States military had dropped an atomic bomb on Hiroshima, Japan, and caused massive destruction. The news reports stated that the uranium from the bomb had been made at Clinton Engineering Works in Tennessee. It was the first time the residents of Oak Ridge understood the full extent of their project.

After the war, the residents learned that there two other secret cities built in the U.S. One was in in Hanford, WA, where plutonium was made for the bomb dropped on Nagasaki, and the third city was in Los Alamos, NM, where the bombs were assembled. The residents of all three cities had kept their work secret from the entire world.

On August 15, Japan announced its surrender to the Allies. The atomic bombs dropped on Japan are the only nuclear weapons that have been used in war to this day.

Elza Gate Military Police in 1945.

The American Navy man couldn't believe what he saw in his spy glass. Was that really a Japanese submarine? It couldn't be. Could it? The Japanese couldn't have made it all the way to San Francisco. But a few nights later, another Japanese submarine surfaced off the coast of Santa Barbara, CA, and fired shells at an oil storage facility. Were the Japanese planning to invade California?

America couldn't take any chances; they had to prepare for the worst. Pearl Harbor had been bombed just 2 months before. The West Coast of the United States was home to important military bases and manufacturing plants. They had to be protected. It was time for Operation Camouflage California.

Lieutenant General John L. De Witt, Head of Western Defense Command, was given the huge task of hiding the factories and military bases of California. But how do you hide enormous airplane runways, giant manufacturing plants, and barracks full of soldiers? With a little help from Hollywood.

Set designers, special effects people, carpenters, and lighting experts volunteered to help. The plan was to change how California looked from the air so that Japanese pilots would not be able to see the actual location of the bases and factories.

First, the set designers created fake airfields in the middle of empty pastures. They burned the grass in long rectangular strips so that, from the air, the dark strips looked like runways.

They built fake barracks out of plywood and painted canvas. The Goodyear Company supplied inflated rubber models of airplanes.

To hide the California Lockheed Vega Aircraft plant, the gigantic building and its parking lots were all hidden underneath a fake "suburb." The set designers stretched a huge canopy of chicken wire and canvas over the top of the entire area. The wire was held up with poles and scaffolds and at the edges it sloped down like a tent to blend in with the ground. Painters came in and drew roads, sidewalks, and squares of green lawn. They built fake canvas houses and "planted" fake trees. Fake cars and trucks were place on the fake streets and clotheslines were put in the yards. Real clothes hanging on the line fluttered in the breeze. From the air it looked like a typical California suburb.

Trees were constructed out of chicken wire frames coated with a sticky adhesive. Feathers were spray painted green and attached to the "tree branches." The feathers would move in the wind like real tree leaves.

To maintain the illusion of a real live neighborhood, workers had to periodically move the fake cars and trucks and take in the laundry and put out new clothes. They climbed up the scaffolding and walked on special catwalks high above the factory rooftop to move the props and fix any trees or shrubs that might have fallen over.

To test the success of the disguise, a pilot took a visiting War Department general on a plane ride over the Lockheed plant. The general thought the town looked nice, but wanted to know where the airplane factory was. The camouflage was a success.

All along the Pacific Coast, airplane factories and military bases were disguised. In Seattle, the 26-acre Boeing plant was covered up by an entire fake town that included shops, municipal buildings, schools, and parks.

Before

The Lockheed aircraft factory at Burbank was one of the key facilities to be disguised in case of a Japanese aerial bombardment.

After

As you can see in the picture above, it would have made a fairly obvious target. But this is how it looked when Hollywood had finished with it.

Underneath It All

The Lockheed-Vega aircraft plant in Burbank was fully hidden beneath a complete suburb.

When the Allies defeated Japan in the Battle of Midway, United States military leaders believed the West Coast was safe from Japanese attack and the camouflage was taken down. It was the biggest set Hollywood ever made.

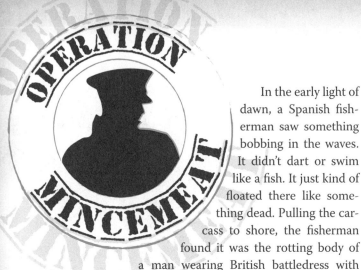

In the early light of dawn, a Spanish fisherman saw something bobbing in the waves. It didn't dart or swim like a fish. It just kind of floated there like something dead. Pulling the carcass to shore, the fisherman found it was the rotting body of a man wearing British battledress with a briefcase chained to his wrist. The fisherman immediately called the authorities and the Spanish military. They collected the body and took it back to headquarters.

After examining the man's uniform to make sure it was authentic and reading all of the letters in the briefcase, the Spanish were sure this was a major in the British Royal Marines who had been killed at sea and had luckily washed up on their shore. Although the Spanish government was officially neutral in the war, many Spanish soldiers and administrators were sympathetic to Germany. The Spanish officials were excited to give this information to their Nazi friends.

The British were furious with the Spanish government. They told the officials that they needed the briefcase back and tried unsuccessfully to get it returned. The Nazi spy network was thrilled. They carefully examined the body and found a wallet that identified the man as Major William Martin of Britain's Royal Marines. He kept letters from his sweetheart in his wallet, a few British pounds, and a receipt for an engagement ring.

The real find was inside the briefcase. Among several official documents was a letter addressed to a senior British officer in Tunisia, Africa. The letter told about plans for the Allied Army to cross the Mediterranean Sea from North Africa to attack German-held Greece and Sardinia.

This was important information, but what if the British were trying to fool the Germans? What if this was all a trick? German spies checked British casualty lists in *The Times of London* newspaper and found Major Martin was listed as killed at sea. The information from England matched the body they had in custody. The German officials decided the information was true and informed Hitler of their amazing find.

With this information, Adolf Hitler moved his troops from France to Greece so that they would be ready to fight off the invasion of Allied troops. But the Allied invasion never came through Greece. Instead the Allies marched in from Sicily and rolled through Italy with very few troops to fight them. Most of the German Army waited for nothing in Greece. Hitler and the Nazis had been fooled.

The man who had washed up on the shore of Spain was part of Operation Mincemeat. Two British Officers, Charles Cholmondeley and Ewen Montagu, members of the XX committee (double cross committee), had come up with the idea of using a dead body as a decoy to fool the Nazis. At first they thought about attaching a body to a parachute and dropping it over enemy lines, but they didn't think they could keep the body fresh enough to fool the Germans into thinking it was a real accident. They finally decided to launch the body out to sea. Dead bodies tended to rot in the water, so the Germans would not be so suspicious.

They obtained a body from the morgue and had papers forged on Royal Navy stationery. With the help of other British intelligence officers, they made sure that every detail of the decoy was correct. They gave him forged identification papers and Royal Navy documents. They even had a secretary write fake love letters from his pretend fiancée. They also made sure he was dressed in the correct style of uniform, right down to regulation underwear.

Spy gadget maker, Charles Fraser-Smith, designed a steel canister to hold the body. The canister was filled with dry ice

OPERATION SARDINE

The Norway fishermen were furious when they found out their prime sardine catch was being confiscated by the Nazis, so they came up with a plan to use the sardines as weapon. They asked the British to send them all the croton oil they could find. (Croton oil is a powerful laxative.) The sardines were soaked in the oil and shipped to Nazi submarines. For a few days, Operation Sardine brought the Nazi Navy to their knees, or at least the bathroom.

to keep the body from decomposing further. Then the canister, loaded with the body, was put on the British submarine HMS Seraph. The submarine transported the body to a point about a mile off the coast of Spain where naval officers knew that the tides would wash the body ashore. There they threw the body into the ocean and let the waves do the rest of the work.

Operation Mincemeat was such a success that the German Army waited in Greece for 2 weeks looking for the invasion that never came. By keeping the German Army out of Italy, it helped the Allies take back the European front.

SPY TRAINING

Book Safe

Once you have been given instructions for a secret operation you need to be able to hide your plans. That's why you need to build a book safe.

Materials:

❑ An adult assistant (yeah, you might have to let someone in on your secret!)

❑ Old book (get an adult's permission to use the book first)

❑ Pencil

❑ Ruler

❑ Mat knife (to used only by the adult assistant!)

Open the book close to the beginning, but not on the first page. You need some uncut pages. With a pencil and ruler, draw a rectangle on the page. Be careful to leave page margins around the rectangle.

Ask your adult assistant to use the knife to cut through the pages of the book. Once your assistant has cut through the pages, you can remove them. You should have a hollowed out rectangle in your book. This is where you can hide all of your secret documents. And if you really want to fool somebody, store the book with other books on your shelf. They won't know one is actually a safe!

Ballpoint Pen Message Holder

Need to get secret information to a fellow spy? You need to make a ballpoint pen message holder. It's super easy and no one will ever know that when you loan your friend a pen, you are actually passing secret messages.

Materials:

- ❑ Old ballpoint pen (find one that does not have a clear cylinder)
- ❑ Small slip of paper

Dearest Mother,

The Germans have _____ an extra letter home each month
APR BR BR _____ R MWEKR PAAWS TZJGA AQYIV
RGEL _____ WCLP EESEM HGJJI. Please go to the Church on
_____ say ambidextrous tractor wanderlust lumbago underground _____ndant xylophone.

Love your son,
Jackson

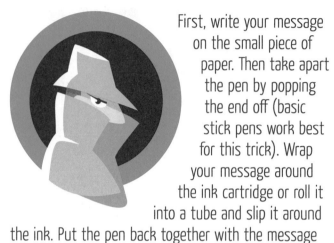

First, write your message on the small piece of paper. Then take apart the pen by popping the end off (basic stick pens work best for this trick). Wrap your message around the ink cartridge or roll it into a tube and slip it around the ink. Put the pen back together with the message inside. You now have an easy way to pass secret information!

SECRET

WEAPONS

DOODLEBUGS

FU-GO KU-GO NO-GO

RAT BOMBS

BAT BOMBS

MUFFIN BOMBS

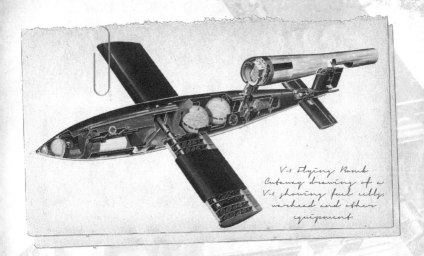

V-1 Flying Bomb
Cutaway drawing of a
V-1 showing fuel cells,
warhead and other
equipment

DOODLEBUGS

Known as a buzz bomb or a doodlebug, the V-1 flying bomb was a German secret weapon that struck fear into the hearts of the people of Great Britain. Allied planes had photographed strange-looking German launch sites and intelligence officers suspected that the Germans were working on some type of rocket.

One week after the Allies' Normandy invasion of 1945, Germany unleashed the V-1 flying bombs on Britain. The V came from the German word Vergeltungswaffen, meaning weapon of reprisal or revenge. The motor on the bombs made a loud buzzing sound that people could hear on the ground. As the bomb got closer to its target, the motor stopped and the bomb glided silently until it hit the target and exploded. British people learned to listen for the buzzing sound of the doodlebugs. If the doodlebug was buzzing as it passed over, you were safe. If it was silent, you were in trouble.

The doodlebug was a weapon the world had never seen before. The Allies had experimented with the possibility of unmanned airplanes flying into enemy territory loaded with explosives, but they had not developed anything like the V-1 rocket.

During the first campaign, the Nazis launched 100 doodlebug rockets every hour. During an 80-day period, 6,000 British civilians were killed, 17,000 were wounded, and more than a million buildings were destroyed. It was truly a weapon of revenge.

The Allies scrambled to find a way to stop the devastation caused by the horrible doodlebugs. They tried shooting down the bombs with anti-aircraft guns. But the bombs were too high in the air and too tiny of a target for accurate shooting. The doodlebug bombs flew too low for airplanes to be able to shoot at them.

The British put up more than 2,000 barrage balloons around London. A barrage was a large balloon held in place by steel cables. It was hoped that the doodlebugs would hit the cables and explode before they could hit a building. But the doodlebugs' wings were equipped with cable cutters. Only about 300 doodlebugs were stopped by the barrage balloons.

The only way the Allies could defeat the doodlebug was to capture the launch sites. As the Allies continued to fight their way across France and into Germany, they captured more and more of the launch sites until the last launch site was taken over on March 29, 1945. The Nazis surrendered to the Allies on May 8, 1945.

Vortex Gun

Nazi scientists invented a cannon that launched large shells made of coal dust and slow-burning explosives high into the air. The mix of heated air and coal dust would create a wind vortex that was so strong it could destroy planes and create small tornadoes. Unfortunately for the Nazis, they couldn't get the Vortex Gun to hit the right target very often so they never used it in combat.

FU-GO
KU-GO
NO-GO

BALLOON BOMBS AND DEATH RAYS
are usually part of science fiction movies,
but during World War II, Japanese scientists
worked on both of these projects and
several other fantastical weapons.

Desperate to attack the mainland of the United States, Japanese scientists launched Operation Fu-Go. The Fu-Go (fire balloon) was a huge hydrogen balloon loaded with incendiary (fire making) bombs. The plan was to release the balloons into the jet stream over the Pacific Ocean. The direction of the air currents would float the balloons directly to the west coast of the United States and Canada. When they landed, the bombs would go off and start fires in West Coast cities. It seemed like a good plan, but it didn't work.

Between November 1944 and April 1945, Japan launched more than 9,300 Fu-Go balloons. It is estimated that only about 300 balloons ever reached North America. Most of the balloons dropped harmlessly in the Pacific Ocean. A few reached the coast of Oregon and some drifted inland as far as Kansas, Iowa, and Manitoba, Canada.

Some cowboys in Nevada discovered one of the Fu-Go balloons that had harmlessly exploded. They cut up the silk cloth and used it as a hay tarp. A prospector near Elko, NV, found one and loaded it on his donkey to deliver it to the local authorities. Soon the United States and Canadian Military knew that Japan had launched another attack on North America.

Fighter pilots were alerted to be on the watch for the balloons, but the balloons flew so high and fast they were impossible to shoot down. Fighter pilots destroyed less than 20 of the balloons.

Sadly one Fu-Go balloon killed six people. Pastor Archie Mitchell and his pregnant wife, Elise, took a Sunday school class on a picnic in a forest in Southern Oregon. As pastor Mitchell parked the car, his wife and the five middle school students looked for a place to lay out their picnic. They spied the balloon and walked toward it. The bomb exploded and killed all six of them. It was the only successful attack on the continental U.S.

The President asked the press to keep the deaths a secret so that the Japanese would not know about their success. Because of the news blackout, the Japanese believed that none of their Fu-Go balloons was successful, so they gave up the program.

The Ku-Go program was the Japanese effort to create a death ray. An article published in *The New York Times* in 1934 caught the attention of some Japanese scientists. Famous inventor Nikola Tesla claimed to have invented a "death-ray device" that could "drop an army in its tracks and bring down squadrons of airplanes 250 miles away." However Tesla never showed anyone the device and it was never proven to exist. That didn't stop Japanese scientists from trying to build their own death ray or Ku-Go.

The Japanese experimented with magnetrons to develop high power microwaves. By the end of the war they claimed to be successful at killing a rabbit from 1,000 yards away. But the rabbit had to be standing perfectly still.

In reality, both the Ku-Go and Fu-Go were a No-Go.

SUN GUN

One of the weapons **German scientists** researched was the Sun Gun. They thought that if they launched **huge mirrors into space**, they could use them to burn cities just like a magnifying glass can be used to scorch a bug. The scientists estimated it would take 50 to 100 years to make the gun operational, so they **scrapped the Sun Gun project**.

RAT BOMBS

British Prime Minister Winston Churchill said that the British people would use every means possible to fight against the Nazi Regime and they did—they even tried fighting with dead rats.

The idea came about because of the ordinary job that janitors had in the 1940s of cleaning up boiler rooms. Often rats or mice would die in the building and the janitor would get rid of the body by throwing it into the boiler room fire. The British SOE thought they could use this daily routine to their advantage.

What if the rats were actually packed with explosives? Then, when the janitor threw the rat body into the fire, it would cause a boiler explosion. Just a small amount of explosive and a steam boiler could explode, potentially taking out a whole power station.

The SOE obtained 100 rats from a medical laboratory. The rats were killed, then cut open and stuffed full of explosives. The rats were then carefully sewn back together so no one would suspect that the dead animal was actually a bomb.

However, the rat bombs were never used. The first shipment of rats was discovered by the Nazis, and Nazi officials exhibited the rat bombs at their top military schools. They conducted extensive searches in factories all over Germany looking for the clever British rat bombs. The British never sent another shipment. They felt they had already been successful by costing the Germans so much time and effort hunting for bombs that weren't there.

Operation Chaff

When is aluminum foil a war weapon? When it is used to jam radars and confuse Nazi planes! During the 1943 Battle of Hamburg, the British dropped bales of aluminum foil strips from their planes. Called Chaff, the foil threw the German radars into total confusion and helped the Allies win the battle. It was so successful that Chaff is still used today to confuse radar readings.

BAT BOMBS

Dr. Lytle Adams was a dentist with an idea for a top-secret weapon: a bat bomb. As a patriotic American, Dr. Adams wanted to help in the fight against the Japanese. He observed that buildings in 1940s Japan were often made of paper, bamboo, and wood. The buildings were highly flammable and a massive fire could wipe out ammunition plants and other military factories. If there were some way to start small fires throughout a Japanese city, it could help bring a faster end to the war.

Bats were the solution, Dr. Adams thought. As nocturnal hibernating animals, they could be released in the dark and would seek out roofs and attics to sleep in during the daylight.

They were also physically capable of carrying a small load of weight. Mother bats often flew carrying their babies. If the military could attach a small bomb-like device, the bats would become tiny arsonists, setting off fires throughout a Japanese city.

Dr. Adams took his idea to his friend, First Lady Eleanor Roosevelt. Mrs. Roosevelt took the plan straight to her husband. President Roosevelt approved the idea and sent it out for army testing. They developed a tiny incendiary (fire-making) device that could be attached to each bat. A special bat carrier was made to hold the animals as they were being transported by airplane. The bat carriers looked like a bomb casing and had compartments for 40 bats.

The plan was to drop the bat bombs from 5,000 feet. There would be a parachute attached to the bombs that would open at 1,000 feet and the bats would be released to find their hiding spots. The military believed that 10 B-24 bombers could fly from Alaska and drop more than a million bat bombs on the industrial cities of Japan.

Bats were captured from sites in New Mexico and taken to be used in tests conducted by the military. The tests were successful. The bats could indeed cause fires. As a matter of fact, when some of the bats escaped, they set the Carlsbad Army Field on fire! But the bat bomb program was canceled in 1944 because officials thought the testing was taking too long. They wanted a quicker end to the war, and they believed the atomic bomb project would be faster and more efficient.

Dr. Adams always believed that the bat bombs would have been effective without all of the devastation brought about with the radiation poisoning from the atomic bomb. He said, "Think of thousands of fires breaking out simultaneously over a circle of 40 miles in diameter for every bomb dropped. Japan could have been devastated, yet with small loss of life."

History will never know if Dr. Adams was right. The atomic bomb was dropped over Hiroshima on August 6, 1945.

MUFFIN BOMBS

How do you fight the Japanese Army? With exploding muffins of course!

After the Japanese bombed Pearl Harbor and declared war on the United States, the Americans partnered with the Chinese to fight against the Japanese Empire. The Chinese lacked weapons and explosives. America had them, but shipping them to the Chinese was next to impossible. The Germans and the Japanese would never let ships full of guns and explosives get through to China . . . but they would allow shipments of food.

What if the explosives looked like food? American soldier George Bogdan began experimenting with baking flour and mixed it with a highly explosive chemical called HMX. George's lethal mixture could actually be used by a cook to bake muffins, pancakes, or bread. When it was baked, it smelled and looked just like regular bread. And it could be eaten, although there were some terrible side effects for the person who ate it—massive stomach cramps and intense vomiting.

The explosive flour was packaged in regular flour bags and could be smuggled past Japanese checkpoints to the Chinese resistance fighters. If the smuggler was caught with the explosive flour, he could whip up some not-so-tasty muffins and eat one in front of the Japanese soldier. No one would suspect that the flour was an explosive until later when the smuggler began to vomit. Of course, by that time the smuggler hoped to be too far away for possible capture.

When he was in China, demolitionist Frank Gleason wanted to demonstrate how easy it was to bake a biscuit, put a blasting cap in it, and blow something up:

> So I told this Chinese cook at Happy Valley to make some muffins out of the explosive flour. I said, "Do not eat those muffins! They are poison. Do not eat them!" You should have seen them when they came out of the oven. They were gorgeous. The cook thought to himself, "Those . . . Americans just want those muffins for themselves!" He violated what I told him and he ate one. He almost died.

Julia Child
OSS Agent

Before world famous chef Julia Child was cooking up quiche and soufflé, she was mixing up secret shark repellent for the Office of Strategic Services. Her concoction was painted on explosives that were targeting German U-boats. Before Julia helped invent the shark repellent, curious sharks would nose the explosives and sometimes set them off before they could damage the enemy boats.

Modifications were made to the chemical composition of the explosive to make it less toxic. It would never be good for anyone to eat a whole loaf of explosive bread, but at least it was less gut-wrenching.

The exploding muffins were a success and during World War II, 15 tons of the explosive flour was smuggled into China and used to fight the Japanese.

Spy Rocket

You can build and launch your own spy rocket using easy to find materials.

Materials:

- ❏ Printer paper
- ❏ Clear tape
- ❏ Scissors
- ❏ Pencil
- ❏ Straw (slightly thinner than the pencil)

Cut a rectangular strip of paper about 1 1/2 inches wide and 4 1/2 inches long. Roll the paper tightly around the pencil and tape along the long edge. Fold over one end of the tube into a cone shape and secure with tape.

Remove the pencil and blow gently into the open end of the paper rocket. Is any air escaping? Use more tape to seal the leaks.

Cut out and fold two sets of fins using the pattern below. Tape the fins near the open end of the cylinder. Place the straw inside the open end of the rocket. Leave some of the straw sticking out so you can hold it.

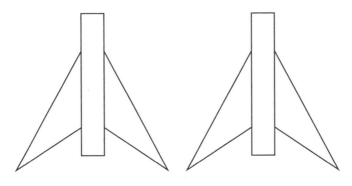

Blow on the straw to launch your rocket. You can experiment with your rocket just like the scientists of World War II. Try changing the design of the fins to make your rocket go farther and higher.

Balloon Flour Bomb

Bombs are extremely dangerous and they are not something anyone should try to experiment with. To get an idea of how much impact a bomb can have, you can test a flour bomb.

Materials:

- ❑ Large outdoor space
- ❑ Flour
- ❑ Balloons
- ❑ Tablespoon

Before you inflate your balloons, place 2–3 tablespoons of flour into the balloon. Then fully inflate the balloon and tie it off. Take your balloon outside and throw it onto the ground. When the balloon explodes, look at where the flour splatters. The flour makes an impression much larger than the original balloon. This is why explosives can be so destructive—they cause damage much larger than just the size of the bomb.

3D SPYING

The spies of World War II did not have modern tools like satellite images, spy drones, or even Google Earth. Locating the movements of enemy troops was a complicated process that involved spy planes, giant cameras, and 3D glasses.

For 8 months in 1940, Nazi Germany pounded the Allied forces with air raids, raining bombs on Britain and killing more than 40,000 civilians. The Allies were desperate to change the course of the war and came up with a daring spy plan. Engineers took the fast flying spitfire fighter plane and altered the engine so it could fly higher. They stripped off the guns and fitted the plane with five state-of-the-art cameras. Each camera was more than 2 feet long with a 6-inch lens.

The spitfire pilots were given maps and ordered to fly into enemy territory and take pictures—lots and lots of pictures. It was dangerous duty. Because of the weight of the cameras, the guns were removed from the plane. Pilots had no defensive weapons and they were flying straight into enemy camps. If they were shot down or caught, it would not only cost them their lives, but the Nazis would learn about the Allies' spy program as well. But it was a risk they had to take. The pilots were successful, and for 2 years, spy planes raced high above the clouds in Germany snapping millions of pictures.

Once the film was developed, it was given to men and women who spent hours poring over the photos through spectrometers, or special 3D glasses. The photographs were overlaid on top of each other so that with special glasses the analysts could see the shadows and depth of the photos.

With the aid of 3D glasses, the analysts were able to see the difference between fake decoy ships the Germans had placed near their harbors and where the real ships were anchored. They were able to see when fields were being turned into landing strips and airfields. Most important of all, they were able to discover a strange tall weapon they had never seen before. It was a V-1 rocket—the first rockets ever used as weapons.

PINK PLANES

Some of the toughest pilots in WWII flew in pink planes. Spitfire planes were often used for spy missions, and they were painted pink because the missions usually took place toward sundown. This way the planes blended with the pinkish tint of sunset.

THE NIGHT WITCHES

They were silent as death and twice as frightening. The Russian Nachthexen, or Night Witches, as the Germans named them, were the stuff of Nazi nightmares. Every night they flew quietly through the air, raining bombs on supply depots, base camps, and armories. Nothing stopped them. They flew in total darkness and in all kinds of weather. The Germans thought the Russians must have injected their pilots with some super drug that made them see in the dark, or else they really had magical powers.

Commando: Operation Nachthexen, No 4599
Story: Mac MacDonald Art: Carlos Pino

In reality, the night witches were young Russian women, some of them still teenagers. They were an elite group of bomber pilots who flew more than 23,000 missions and dropped more than 3,000 pounds of bombs. They were the first women combat pilots in the world.

They attacked in silence because the women pilots actually cut their engines as they approached their targets and glided on air to drop their bombs. The only sound the Germans heard was the wind rushing through their wood and canvas wings. The Germans said it was the noise of witches' brooms flying through the air.

Their leader was Marina Raskova, a record-breaking pilot. She was as famous in Russia as Amelia Earhart was in the United States. When Germany invaded Russia in 1941, the Russian government asked Raskova to organize a regiment of women pilots to fly night combat missions. These young pilots were to target German supply areas and were given slow speed Po-2 biplanes. They were made of canvas and plywood, and the fastest these planes could fly was 82 knots, or 94 miles per hour. This was slower than most of the planes that had been used in World War I, so all of the German planes could outrun the Night Witches. What they couldn't do was outmaneuver them.

The slow-flying Po-2 plane could make tight turns without stalling and could fly low to the ground. Sometimes the Witches flew so low they could hide behind hedgerows. The German pilots had a terrible time trying to shoot them down. The Night Witches would fly close to their target, then cut their engines to reduce the noise. After they dropped their bombs, they would start the engines and fly away. The first clue the Germans had that a bomb was coming was the sound of the engine starting back up. By that time it was too late.

At its largest, the Night Witches regiment had 40 two-person crews. Their antique planes lacked basic instruments. They had no radios, and the pilots were not given parachutes. The parachutes wouldn't have done any good because they flew too low for the chute to open.

They had to navigate their targets using a stopwatch and a map, and the planes were so small that they could only carry two bombs at a time. That meant the pilots had to carry out multiple missions each night. Some nights they went on as many as 18 missions.

The Witches were very successful in their harassment of the Germans; so much that the German military announced that any soldier who shot down a Nachthexen would be awarded the high honor of the Iron Cross. In order to locate the Witches, the Germans used a series of searchlights shining in the air and machine guns firing from the ground. The Po-2 biplanes were ripped to shreds from the gunfire, and several of

Captain Mariya Dolina was a Soviet pilot, squadron commander of the 125th "Marina N. Raskova" Borisov Guards dive bomber Regiment. She was active primarily on the 1st Baltic Front during World War II. On August 18, 1945, Dolina was awarded the title of the Hero of the Soviet Union.

the pilots lost their lives flying for their country. Still, this did not stop the Night Witches.

They developed a system where three biplanes would fly together. Two of the planes would fly directly into the searchlight and the third plane would separate and fly away. Then it would circle back to drop the bombs while the other two planes were taking German fire. The first pilot would drop her bombs and then fly back to her partners. Then they would switch places until all three planes had dropped their payload. It took a great deal of bravery to act as a decoy and willingly attract enemy fire, but it usually worked.

Nadezhda Popova was one of the first young women to enlist, and she flew more than 1,000 missions during WWII. In a 2003 interview, she recalled that on her first mission two of her friends were shot down and killed. She was ordered to go back out on another flight the same night. She did as she was ordered and continued flying until the end of the war. She had many narrow escapes, and one time she counted 42 bullet holes on her plane from just one raid.

Popova died at the age of 91, and as she got older she understood what an amazing feat the Night Witches had pulled off. In a 2010 interview, she said, "I can still imagine myself as a young girl, up there in my little bomber. And I ask myself, 'Nadia, how did you do it?'"

At the end of the war, 23 airwomen of the Night Witches regiment were awarded the Gold Star of the Hero of the Soviet Union. It was the most highly decorated regiment in the entire Soviet Air Force: Each pilot had flown at least 1,000 missions. The 588th Regiment also earned the respect of pilots from other countries. The Free French pilots, who often fought alongside the Night Witches, paid the women this tribute: "Even if it were possible to gather and place at your feet all the flowers on earth, this would not constitute sufficient tribute to your valor."

THE DEVIL'S BRIGADE

They scaled the mountain in pouring rain, tied together to climb up the sheer face of a 600-foot cliff, their faces painted black with shoe polish. Mortars exploded above them, making the sky so orange that one of the soldiers said he felt they were climbing into Hell. They were the men of the Devil's Brigade— the First Special Service Force—and they were trained to do the most impossible missions.

Started in 1943, the Devil's Brigade was a joint operation between the American and Canadian military. Each army sent its best men to receive special training in parachuting, enemy weapons, skiing, rock climbing, and explosives. The soldiers were given nearly double the physical exercise of regular infantry and were expected to know how to assemble and shoot every enemy weapon as well as their own. It was all necessary if they were to survive their missions.

These soldiers parachuted behind enemy lines and were told to capture strongholds of the Nazis. They often had to do

tasks that seemed nearly impossible, like climb that 600-foot cliff to launch a surprise attack on the German Army. They were dropped on glaciers and had to ski down mountains and then fight a battle. They were sent to Italy to beat back the German lines in Anzio and make a path for the Allied Army.

When they were in Anzio, the Nazi leaders warned their soldiers that they would be fighting an elite Canadian-American force that was "treacherous, unmerciful, and clever." The first Nazi soldier who captured one of the Devil's Brigade was promised a 10-day furlough. The men from the Devil's Brigade refused to be taken alive. They fought so fiercely that the Germans thought there were 10 times as many men in the Devil's Brigade as there actually was.

After the war, the men of the Devil's Brigade were awarded every medal imaginable, including the Distinguished Unit Award for extraordinary valor. The 1,800 man unit accounted for 12,000 Nazi casualties and captured more than 7,000 prisoners.

1,800 man unit
12,000 Nazi casualties
7,000 prisoners

The Brigade was disbanded at the end of the war, but because of the great success of the specially trained soldiers, the United States developed the Army Special Forces unit that later became known as the Green Berets. Today it is still one of the most elite fighting forces in the world.

THE CASE OF CORPORAL WOJTEK

Corporal Wojtek was an outstanding soldier in the Polish Army, even if he was a little hairy. The **famous soldier** served as a munitions carrier during the battle of Monte Cassino and never dropped a single crate, which was **pretty amazing** since Corporal Wojtek was a bear.

After the war he retired to the Edinburgh Zoo in Scotland, where **thousands of people visited** the bear that went undercover as a soldier.

First 29 Navajo U.S. Marine Corps code-talker recruits being sworn in at Fort Wingate, NM.

CODE TALKERS

Codes were critical to military success and finding a code that could not be broken was the goal of every military leader. During World War I, an army captain overheard two of his men speaking to each other in a language he could not understand. The men were Solomon Louis and Mitchell Bobb, and they were talking in the Choctaw language.

The captain saw the advantage of using the Native American language as a code. It was a language that was in limited use outside the Choctaw nation, and it was mainly oral. Without a written record of the words, it would be extremely difficult for code breakers to decipher.

The successful use of the Choctaw language was discovered by the Germans after the war. So before the start of his European invasion, Adolf Hitler sent a team of 30 German anthropologists to the United States to learn and record Native American languages. But the Germans found that the languages were just too complex to understand. They left the United States without ever fully understanding any of the languages.

When America entered the war in 1941, a World War I veteran, Phillip Johnston, suggested that the use of Native American language be revived for codes. As the child of missionaries, Johnston had grown up living with the Navajo people and spoke the language fluently. He met with major General Clayton B. Vogel and explained that the extremely complex Navajo language would be ideal for developing an unbreakable code.

Johnston even staged demonstrations and showed that the Navajos could encode, transmit, and decode a three-line English message in 20 seconds. It took a military decoding machine 30 minutes to do the same task. The military was so impressed that in 2 weeks they recruited 29 Navajos to develop a code using their language. By the end of the war, there were Code Talkers from 16 different tribes. They served around the world in the Army, Navy, and Marines.

Men recruited to be code talkers were sent to a special school where they learned how to be radio operators, how to transmit code, handle weapons, and repair radios. For everyday communication, the code talkers simply spoke to each other in their native language. But for top-secret messages they developed a special code know as Type One code.

The Navajo Code Talkers selected a word from their language to represent each letter of the English alphabet. Each letter of the English alphabet had more than one Navajo word assigned to it so that it would be harder to break the code, for example:

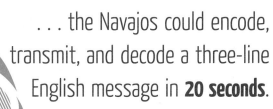

. . . the Navajos could encode, transmit, and decode a three-line English message in **20 seconds**. It took a military decoding machine **30 minutes** to do the same task.

Alphabet	Navajo Word
A	Wol-la-chee
A	Be-la-sana
A	Tse-nill

Any of the three Navajo words could represent the letter A. Even if someone understood the Navajo language they would not be able to understand what was being said. To make it even more complicated, they selected some words and military terms and gave them Navajo words, for example:

English Word	Navajo Word	Literal Translation
Navy	Tal-kah-silago	Sea soldier
River	Toh-yil-kal	Much water
Sniper	Oh-behi	Pick 'em off
Tank	Chay-da-gahi	Tortoise
Tank destroyer	Chay-da-gahi-nail-tsaidi	Tortoise killer

The Code Talkers memorized all 17 pages of their code. Everything needed to decode a message was kept in their head. Many of the military trainers were amazed at their ability to memorize. The Navajo explained that theirs was an oral language, and they had been taught from childhood to memorize all of their stories and histories. It was a skill that served them well on the battlefields of World War II.

The code talkers were sent to fight the Japanese in the Pacific theatre. They handled all major battlefield communications. Not a single message was deciphered. In the final battle of the war, at Iwo Jima, they sent more than 800 critical messages. It is hard to estimate the number of lives that were saved by the Code Talkers, but it is certain that they helped the Allies win the war.

Everything needed to decode a message was kept in their head. Many of the **military trainers were amazed** at their ability to memorize.

Build a Glider

You can build a model of a glider to see how the night witches used their planes to terrorize the Nazis.

Materials:
- ❏ Masking tape
- ❏ Scissors
- ❏ Styrofoam plates or take-out container
- ❏ Drinking straws
- ❏ Plane pattern
- ❏ Pen
- ❏ Clay

Use the pen to trace the wing and body pattern of the glider onto the Styrofoam. Cut out the parts of the wings and tape them together. The drinking straw will be the body of the glider. Tape the wings to the front of the straw. Tape the tail and rudder to the back of the straw. Put a small amount of clay on the nose of the glider to give it some weight. You may need to experiment to see what amount of clay is right for your wind conditions. Now you are now ready to launch your glider.

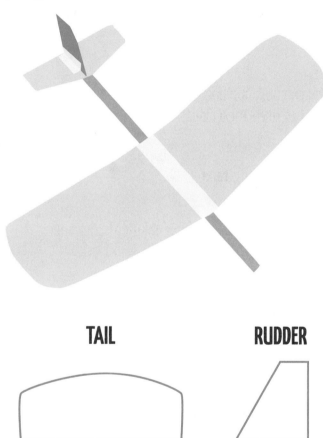

TAIL

RUDDER

WINGS

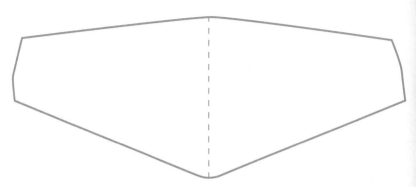

Note: Using just two foam plates and splicing in the middle, it is possible to make this wing with a double taper. Looks like a good wing for a jet aircraft.

Note: This wing is made from just two plates by creating a straight center section from one plate and the two tip pieces from another plate. With no joint in the middle this should make for a stronger wing.

SPY TRAINING

3D Spy Glasses

World War II spies used special lenses to look at the pictures taken by the 3D pilots, but you can make your own 3D glasses with cardboard and plastic.

Materials:

❑ Cardboard

❑ Scissors

❑ Clear tape

❑ Sheet of plastic
(suggestions: cellophane, transparency sheet, mylar, or acetate)

❑ Red and blue permanent markers

❑ Pattern for glasses frame and lenses

Trace the glasses pattern onto the cardboard then cut out the pieces. Trace the pattern for the lenses onto the plastic and cut them out. Color one lens blue and the other lens red. Tape the lenses inside the openings of the glasses. Your glasses are ready for 3D spying.

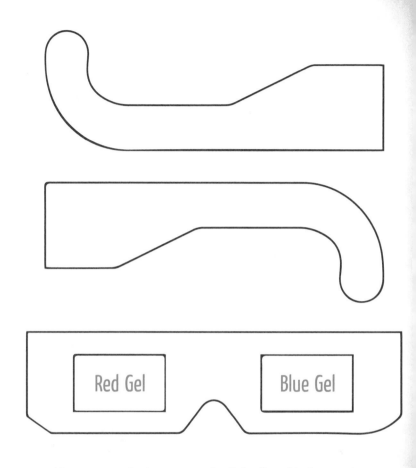

Red Gel

Blue Gel

View some 3D pictures at the links listed below and see what you discover!

» http://senoptium.my/watching-anaglyph-images-with-your-own-3d-glasses/#.UxpWw2CYbcs

» http://stereo.gsfc.nasa.gov/classroom/3d.shtml

» http://en.wikipedia.org/wiki/File:3-d_anaglyph_of_Zagreb_(2007).jpg

SPY TRAINING

Code Talkers' Challenge

Use the Navajo Code Talkers' dictionary to solve this
message:

> Gloe-ih ah-jah tsah dzeh ah-nah be
> tse-gah ah-jah dibeh-yazzie cla-gi-aih.

Share the dictionary with a friend to write your own
coded messages.

Navajo Indian communication men with the Marines on Saipan landed with the first
assault waves to hit the beach.

Alphabet	Navajo Word	Literal Translation
A	Wol-la-chee	Ant
A	Be-la-sana	Apple
A	Tse-nill	Axe
B	Na-hash-chid	Badger
B	Shush	Bear
B	Toish-jeh	Barrel
C	Moasi	Cat
C	Tla-gin	Coal
C	Ba-goshi	Cow
D	Be	Deer
D	Chindi	Devil
D	Lha-cha-eh	Dog
E	Ah-jah	Ear
E	Dzeh	Elk
E	Ah-nah	Eye
F	Chuo	Fir
F	Tsa-e-donin-ee	Fly
F	Ma-e	Fox
G	Ah-tad	Girl
G	Klizzie	Goat
G	Jeha	Gum
H	Tse-gah	Hair

Alphabet	Navajo Word	Literal Translation
H	Cha	Hat
H	Lin	Horse
I	Tkin	Ice
I	Yeh-hes	Itch
I	A-chi	Intestine
J	Ah-ya-tsinne	Jaw
J	Yil-doi	Jerk
K	Jad-ho-loni	Kettle
K	Ba-ah-ne-di-tinin	Key
K	Klizzie-yazzie	Kid
L	Dibeh-yazzie	Lamb
L	Ah-jad	Leg
L	Nash-doie-tso	Lion
M	Tsin-tliti	Match
M	Be-tas-tni	Mirror
M	Na-as-tso-si	Mouse
N	Tsah	Needle
N	A-chin	Nose
O	A-kha	Oil
O	Tlo-chin	Onion
O	Ne-ahs-jah	Owl
P	Cla-gi-aih	Pant

Alphabet	Navajo Word	Literal Translation
P	Bi-so-dih	Pig
P	Ne-zhoni	Pretty
Q	Ca-yeilth	Quiver
R	Gah	Rabbit
R	Dah-nes-tsa	Ram
R	Ah-losz	Rice
S	Dibeh	Sheep
S	Klesh	Snake
T	D-ah	Tea
T	A-who	Tooth
T	Than-zie	Turkey
U	Shi-da	Uncle
U	No-da-ih	Ute
V	A-keh-di-glini	Victor
W	Gloe-ih	Weasel
X	Al-na-as-dzoh	Cross
Y	Tsah-as-zih	Yucca
Z	Besh-do-tliz	Zinc

(Answer: We need help.)

Foreign Minister Mamoru Shigemitsu signs the Instrument of Surrender on behalf of the Japanese government during formal surrender ceremonies on the USS MISSOURI in Tokyo Bay, September 2, 1945.

BIBLIOGRAPHY

Books

Atwood, K. J. (2010). *Women heroes of World War II*. Chicago, IL: Chicago Review Press.

Beyer, R. (2003). *The greatest stories never told: Tales from history to astonish bewilder, and stupefy*. New York, NY: Harper.

Beyer, R. (2005). *The greatest war stories never told: 100 tales from military history*. New York, NY: Harper.

Bruer, W. B. (2001). *Deceptions of World War II*. New York, NY: Wiley & Sons.

Bruer, W. B. (2002). *Secret weapons of World War II*. New York, NY: Wiley & Sons.

Ford, B. J. (2011). *Secret weapons: Technology, science and the race to win World War II*. Oxford, England: Osprey.

Gerard, P. (2002). *Secret soldiers*. New York, NY: Dutton.

Myles, B. (1997). *Night witches: The amazing story of Russia's women pilots in World War II*. Chicago, IL: Chicago Review Press.

Paul, D. A. (1998). *The Navajo Code Talkers*. Pittsburgh, PA: Dorrance.

Ludeke, A. (2012). *Weapons of World War II*. New York, NY: Parragon.

Macintyre, B. (2013). *Double cross: The true story of the D-Day spies*. New York, NY: Broadway.

O'Donnell, P. K. (2004). *Operatives, spies, and saboteurs: The unknown story of World War II's OSS*. New York, NY: Free Press.

Segbag-Montefiore, H. (2004). *Enigma: The battle for the code*. New York, NY: Wiley.

Yenne, B. (2003). *Secret weapons of World War II*. New York, NY: Berkeley.

Websites

Galindo, B. (2013). *10 interesting facts about World War II that you might not know*. Retrieved from http://www. buzzfeed.com/briangalindo/12-interesting-facts-about-world-war-ii-that-you-might-not-k

Grenoble, R. (2013). Nazi 'sun gun' aimed to burn cities using huge space mirrors. *Huffington Post*. http://www. huffingtonpost.com/2013/04/04/nazi-sun-gun-space-mirror_n_3015475.html

Inglis-Arkell, E. (2012). *Why World War II spy planes used pink camouflage*. Retrieved from http://io9.com/5872484/why-world-war-ii-spy-planes-used-pink-camouflage

Irvine, C. (2008). Roald Dahl's seductive work as a British spy. *The Telegraph*. Retrieved from http://www.telegraph. co.uk/news/newstopics/howaboutthat/2655185/Roald-Dahls-seductive-work-as-a-British-spy.html

Izon, L. (n.d.). *Camp X: It's where Ian Fleming trained to be a spy during WWII—then he went on to create James Bond 007*. Retrieved from http://www.canadacool.com/ COOLFACTS/ONTARIO/WhitbyJamesBond.html

Jensen, K. T. (2013). *The scariest secret weapons of World War II.* http://www.mandatory.com/2013/02/15/the-scariest-secret-weapons-of-world-war-ii

Julia Child cooked up double life as spy. (2008). *NBC News.* Retrieved from http://www.nbcnews.com/id/26186498/ns/us_news-security/t/julia-child-cooked-double-life-spy/

Thompson, M. (2013). Amazing gadgets of WWII heroes: From rodent bombs to pipe pistols. *Daily Mirror.* Retrieved from http://www.mirror.co.uk/news/uk-news/imperial-war-museum-horrible-histories-2302966

Top 10 secret military weapons of Nazi Germany. (2013). Retrieved from http://malti001.hubpages.com/hub/Top-10-Secret-Weapons-of-Nazi-Germany

Venning, A. (2012). How a teenage Audrey Hepburn escaped a Nazi brothel . . . and other intriguing stories of how those who went on to become famous survived the last dreadful days of the war. *Daily Mail.* Retrieved from http://www.dailymail.co.uk/femail/article-2126313/Audrey-Hepburn-escaped-Nazi-brothel-Sophia-Loren-survived-days-WW2.html

Waldron, B. (2012). Honoring 'Wojtek' the bear who fought the Nazis. *ABC News.* Retrieved from http://abcnews.go.com/blogs/politics/2012/07/honoring-wojtek-the-bear-who-fought-the-nazis/

ABOUT THE AUTHOR

Stephanie Bearce is a writer, a teacher, and a history detective. She loves tracking down spies and uncovering secret missions from the comfort of her library in St. Charles, MO. When she isn't writing or teaching, Stephanie loves to travel the world and go on adventures with her husband, Darrell.